THE EAGLE CHRISTIAN

Waneta Blosser

THE EAGLE CHRISTIAN

The most complete analogy available on the subject of the Golden Eagle and the life of a Christian.

KENNETH L. PRICE

• OLD FAITHFUL PRESS/WETUMPKA, AL •

COPYRIGHT © 1984 BY KENNETH L. PRICE
ALL RIGHTS RESERVED

PUBLISHED BY
OLD FAITHFUL PRESS
RT. 4 BOX 425-H
WETUMPKA, AL. 36092

This book is dedicated to the Master Eagle Himself who has mothered over me, fed me, thrown me out of the nest, borne me on His wings and taught me how to fly. To the author and finisher of my flight lessons, Jesus Christ.

Acknowledgements

Words are a most powerful tool in the mouth of a skilled orator and a pen in the hands of a skilled writer, yet both forms of communication lack the ability to express my appreciation to my friends and family. Countless times they have borne me on their own wings, covered me with their pinions, endured my squawking and most of all believed in me.

Old Testament references are quoted from the Amplified Version©
Zondervan Corp., New York, New York

New Testament references are quoted from Amplified Version©
Lockman Foundation, LaHabra, CA

The photographs contained in this book were obtained from the following sources:

    Gus Wolf, Augusta, Montana
    U.S. Fish and Wildlife Service
    Cecil W. Storeghton
    Tom Smylie
    Photo Researchers, New York
    Alan Carney

THE EAGLE CHRISTIAN

Contents

Preface
1. The Eagle Through the Ages
2. The Eagle is King
3. The Eagle's Source of Strength
4. The Courting Eagle
5. Eagle Homemaker
6. Lovingkindness of the Eagle
7. Eagle Elementary
8. The Ugly Eaglet
9. Eagle University
10. The Preying Eagle
11. Eagle Eye
12. The Eagle's Enemy
13. The Eagle in Sickness
14. The Lonely Eagle
15. The Eagle in the Storm
16. The Majestic Eagle
    Encounter With an Eagle
    The Years of the Eagle
    Additional Information
    Scripture References
    Resources

AND GOD CREATED
 EVERY WINGED BIRD
 ACCORDING TO ITS KIND...
 AND GOD SAW
  THAT IT WAS GOOD

Preface

God, our Creator has, out of His infinite wisdom, used every available source to reveal Himself and His nature to man. Time and again in the Scripture we see God using the things of nature to reveal Himself or to reveal some divine truth concerning the principles that govern man, the earth or even the universe. In the Scripture, God uses the most basic elements such as gold or silver to illustrate His purity, beauty and holiness. He uses the refining processes of these precious elements to demonstrate the refining process that He is performing in our lives (Zechariah 13:9). Even the natural, carnal man in a paganistic religion esteems these elements to be a gift or revelation from his gods. God describes the moving of His spirit by the moving of the winds (John 3:8). He uses the light of day and the dark of night to reveal the nature of the kingdoms of good and evil (Acts 26:18). One may wonder why God has chosen to reveal Himself in such a way. The answer is quite simple - "For ever since the creation of the world His invisible nature and attributes, that is, His eternal power and divinity have been made intelligible and clearly discernible in and through the things that have been made - His handiworks. So (men) are without excuse - altogether without any defense or justification" (Romans 1:20). That means God has placed in creation everything necessary for man to know that there is a God, that He is a God of love and that He is a God of perfection leaving no reason for men to ignore or deny Him.

At this point we could cite examples from Genesis to Revelation where God used things of nature to reveal, even to the carnal man, the mind and purposes of God. A literarian might call these examples "analogies." I choose to call them divine revelations. However, no one can understand the analogies unless they have some knowledge of both subjects. For instance, to understand the parable of the sower one must have an understanding of the seed, the planting and the need for water and fertilizer. Jesus took great care in discussing each of these in order to reveal to men the planting and maturity of the Word in the soil of men's hearts. The parable of the fisherman, the sacrificial lamb, the vineyard and even Paul's analogy of the athlete are all Scriptural examples clearly set out for men to obtain some divine truth by which to order their lives.

"And God said, let the earth put forth vegetation, plants yielding seed, and the fruit trees yielding fruit each according to its kind, whose seed is in itself, upon the earth. And it was so. The earth brought forth vegetation, plants yielding seed according to their own kind, and trees bearing fruit in which was their seed, each according to its kind. And God saw that it was good - suitable, admirable - and He approved it . . . And God said, Let the waters bring forth abundantly and swarm with living creatures, and let birds fly over the earth in the open expanse of the heavens. God created the great sea monsters and every living creature that moves, which the waters brought forth abundantly according to their kinds, and every winged bird according to its kind. And God saw that it was good - suitable, admirable - and He approved it" (Genesis 1:11,12,20,21). What was it about His handiwork that made the Creator say it was good?

There was a man who came to Jesus and asked, "What good thing shall I do to inherit eternal life?" And Jesus said to him "There is only One who is good . . ." (Matthew 19:16-17). If there is only One who is good then why did God speak over His handiwork and say". . . it is good?" The answer is that creation is good only because it is like God. Herein lies a hidden revelation concerning creation. In the book of Genesis the record of all that was created was sealed forever to be, in part or in whole, a revelation of the One who is good. God made His handiwork to be more than a creation; He made it to be a lesson, a projection of some aspect of Himself.

The psalmist wrote "Consider the ant," Jesus said "Consider the lilies . . . consider the sparrows" and John the Baptist said, "Behold the Lamb" - each one becoming a revelation of God's purpose and nature. In our search to find God and to understand His nature we need but to unfold creation and behold our God.

The golden eagle known as "King of Birds," an ageless symbol of strength, beauty, authority and freedom. *Photo: G. Wolf*

1
The Eagle Through The Ages

And God said, "... let birds fly over the earth in the expanse of the heavens ... and God saw that it was good (Genesis 1:20-21)." As these feathered beauties filled the air, God acknowledged their goodness because He saw in them a portrait of Himself. They were created to reflect His nature, His attributes and His relationship with man. Through the course of this book we will be studying the eagle, which has been called the King of Birds.

For centuries the eagle has been recognized by many nations, kingdoms and empires as the King of Birds. The eagle has been, and is today, an international sign of freedom, strength, immortality and authority. Men have reproduced the image of the eagle on coins, emblems, seals and flags. They have used such names as Eagle Corner, New Eagle, Bald Eagle, Black Eagle, Red Eagle, White Eagle, Golden Eagle, War Eagle, Eagleville, Eagleton and Eaglette to indentify villages, cities, bridges, mills, groves, stations and squares. There are Eagle lakes, Eagle mountains, Eagle rivers, Eagle islands, Eagle forks and Eagle buttes without number. There can be no doubt, there is something special about this bird something so special that the educated and uneducated, the civilized and the uncivilized honor the eagle as the king of birds.

One may wonder why the eagle, and not some other bird, has been given such a place of honor. As we open the Scripture to Ezekiel chapter one and verse ten we discover that it was God who gave such a prestigious position to the eagle.

"As for the likeness of their faces, they each had the face of
a man in front and they four had the face of a lion on the
right side, and they four had the face of an ox on the left
side; they four also had the face of an eagle." Ezekiel 1:10

In this verse and again in the book of Revelation chapter four and verse seven God named man as His underlord, or king, of the earth: He named the ox king of domestic beasts, the lion as the king of wild beasts and the eagle He named as king over all other birds. His title as "King of Birds" was not given to him by men, it was conferred upon him by God. Why? The eagle more than any other bird portrays God. His strength, his beauty, his solemnity, his majesty, his fearlessness and his freedom are all attributes that are Godlike. In fact, in Exodus nineteen and verse four God makes an analogy of the eagle and Himself.

> "You yourselves have seen what I did to the Egyptians, and how I bore you on eagles' wings and brought you to Myself." Exodus 19:4

Here God is revealing some astounding characteristics of His paternal nature which we will discuss in detail later in this book. What we need to focus on now is that God, in His Word, likened Himself to the eagle.

As we unfold the life of these birds we will not only discover things about God, we will also discover things about ourselves. In several places in the Scripture, God speaks of men as having the same attributes as the eagle. Man was created in the image of God; therefore, we too have many things in common with our feathered friends.

As we look more closely at the nature of these birds we will see and appreciate God and come to understand ourselves, our problems, our nature and our potential in a completely different light.

2
The Eagle is King

Throughout the course of this study we will be discussing two types of eagles. These are the two types of eagles most commonly found in the Middle East, the type most often referred to in Scripture. Eagles are members of the Falconiformes family along with harriers, hawks, kite, turkeys and condors.

When the Scripture makes reference to an "eagle," it is referring to the Golden eagle or the Imperial eagle. In the name alone there are already spiritual implications. Gold has been a symbol of divinity in the history of hundreds of different cultures. As the name "Golden" implies divinity to the eagle, it also implies to the "Eagle Christian" that he/she has a divine nature.

"For by these He has granted to us His precious and magnificent promises in order that by them you might become partakers of the **divine nature**, having escaped the corruption that is in the world by lust." II Peter 1:4

The name "Imperial" also has some very strong implications. Imperial means "having supreme authority." The eagle's strength, speed and majesty give him dominion over all other birds and the authority to rule over the heavens. As "Eagle Christians" we have also been given the authority to rule the earth. The Scripture says, "Thou hast made them to be a kingdom and priests to our God and they will reign upon the earth" (Revelation 1:6). Just as the eagle reigns over the heavens so the Christian, walking in the God-given power and authority, reigns over the earth. However, our power and authority are in Christ; that is to say outside of Christ we do not have the ability to reign.

"... those who receive the abundance of grace and of the gift of righteousness will **reign as kings in life through the One, Jesus Christ**." Romans 5:17

The eagle is a bird of the air created to live in the heavens, to have an overview of all that is below him.

A typical golden eagle measuring from 28 to 36 inches from head to tail. Notice the golden crown on the eagle for which it is named. *Photo: U.S. Fish & Wildlife Service*

> "Therefore, holy brethren, partakers of a **heavenly calling**, consider Jesus, the apostle and High Priest of our confession." Hebrews 3:1

God has a heavenly calling for every Christian: a calling that summons us closer to God and farther away from the world; a calling that will give us an overview of our situation, our direction and the oncoming storm so that we may properly choose the right course.

> "Even when we were dead in our transgressions (God) made us alive together with Christ and raised us up with Him, and seated us **with Him in the heavenly places in Christ Jesus**." Ephesians 2:6

God has raised the Eagle Christian up to be a heavenly creature, to be the head and not the tail, to know victory and not defeat. We must now begin to see ourselves as "more than conquerors," we must see ourselves as eagles - majestic, strong and free. ". . . They shall lift their wings and mount up [close to God] as eagles . . ." (Isaiah 40:31).

3
The Eagle's Source of Strength

It has been stated humorously that "you are what you eat," inferring that one's diet affects one's strength and health, which in turn affects one's personality, attitude and outlook on life. In part, I must agree with this line of thinking. Haven't we all been around someone who was dieting and found them to be just a little bit edgier than usual? It is logical that a poor diet means poor health, and poor health means less tolerance to the normal stress of daily living.

Perhaps you thought your cat was a picky eater when compared to your dog or some other pet, but the word "finicky" is a word we must reserve for the eagle. While other birds are willing to eat worms, berries, insects and the carcasses of highway tragedies, this is not true with the eagle. The eagle picks his diet: fish today, squirrel tomorrow, lamb the next day and so on - because the eagle does not rely on what he finds, he finds what he wants.

The eagle actually chooses his diet for the day and then goes to find it. Once finding his meal, he dives down and lays hold of it, crushing the life from it with his strong talons (claws). He then ascends to his nest and pulls the prey apart while it is still warm. These birds will have very little to do with decomposing meat of any sort. In this little bit of information we will see one of the hidden mysteries of the kingdom of God revealed.

First, if we are, in the spriritual sense, what we eat and if our strength lies in our diet, then what are we to eat? A poor spiritual diet means poor spiritual health, and poor spiritual health, in turn affects our spiritual tolerance of the day to day battles of this life. Our spiritual diet could consist of a lot of things - fellowship, sunday school, attending church or, perhaps, reading a Christian novel. All of these could serve as a food source, but the Eagle Christian is a finicky eater. He must discern his appetite and then pursue whatever prey will satisfy. Our spirit man has a great appetite, and hunting and pecking in the dirt will not satisfy this great desire. We must learn to discern the spiritual nutrional value of everything we allow to enter into our spirit. Like the eagle we desire living food.

Hebrews 4:12 says:

> "For the word that God speaks is **alive** and full of **power** making it active, operative, energizing and effective; it is sharper than any two edged sword, penetrating to the dividing line of the breath of life (soul) and [the immortal] spirit and of the joints and marrow [that is the deepest parts of our nature] exposing and sifting and analyzing and judging the very thoughts and purposes of the heart."

The Scripture tells us that the "Word" is alive and full of power. Therefore it should be the main course of every Eagle Christian. In I Corinthians chapter ten verses three and four, Paul, speaking about the children of Israel in the wilderness, said:

> "And all [of them] ate the same **spiritual** (supernaturally given) **food**, and they all drank the same supernaturally given **drink**. For they drank **from a spiritual Rock** which followed them - produced by the sole power of God Himself without natural instrumentality - **and the Rock was Christ.**"

Once again we see God intended for our spirit man to draw his strength from God's very words. Without this living food, the Eagle Christian exposes himself to many dangers. Spiritual weakness is the direct result of poor diet. A sick or weak eagle will not reproduce, he will not be able to discern the truth, nor will he be able to contend with his enemies. For example, let's examine the diet of the eagle's cousin.

The vulture builds his nest in dead trees or even on the ground. His head and neck are featherless and hairless so that he can more readily stick his head into a corrupted carcass. The diet of these birds is a diet of left-overs. After circling over this meal for hours to make sure it's dead, the vulture descends, usually accompanied by others who don't want the solitary lifestyle of the eagle. There is nothing finicky, picky or even tasteful about the vulture's diet. The vulture will eat until he becomes intoxicated with blood by overeating and then is unable to fly, often becoming the prey himself.

Now let's move this story of nature into the spiritual realm. Spiritual vultures are not picky with their diet, they would just as soon watch a horror movie as they would **The Ten Commandments**. They are more likely to attend fellowships where gossip is the main course than they are to seek solitude with their Bibles. The spiritual vulture will gorge himself with so much fellowship, activities and entertainment, he will not be able to fly or endure any type of hardship and so becomes the prey of his enemies.

On the other hand, the Eagle Christian will seek out live prey and draw his strength from the strength of the Word. He will seek out his food in solitude and not involve himself with the corruption of gossip and idleness. The Eagle Christian is the strongest and most beautiful of all Christians because he has found the source of health and strength.

"My son, attend to **my words**; consent and submit to my sayings. Let them not depart from your sight; keep them in the center of your heart. For they **are life** to those who find them, **healing and health** to all their flesh." Proverbs 4:20-22

A golden eagle with her catch for the day, a pheasant. Notice how she actually balances herself on her tail feathers while clutching the catch with her talons. *Photo: Photo Researchers*

4
The Courting Eagle

When the eagle is a year old he begins to take care of himself. Having left the security of his parents, he is now out on his own. He has much to learn about being an eagle - flying, hunting and courting. Some time after the eagle has been out on his own (approximately 3 years) he begins to take interest in another bird, a female bird. Spring fever has come to the eagle. It starts with a game of tag that could last for days. Then the female eagle becomes bored with this game so she invents her own. This game, however, is not really her own invention, the eagles have been playing it for centuries.

The game goes something like this: the female makes a dive down to the ground and grabs a stick in her talons, not a very big stick but just something to play with. Then she ascends high up into the sky with the male eagle right on her tail. When she reaches an altitude between eight and ten thousand feet she begins to fly in a three dimensional figure eight with wide circles and curves. The male eagle, still playing tag, is staying right behind her in her peculiar figure eight pattern. All of a sudden, the female drops the stick and the male, being such a gentleman, attempts to retrieve it for her. He breaks the pattern and swoops to catch the stick. After having caught the stick, he attempts to return it; however, the female seems quite uninterested and dives down after a larger stick to play with. The male eagle doesn't take her rejection to heart, he simply returns the stick to the ground and falls in after the female who ascends to an altitude of about six to eight thousand feet to repeat the game. And so this game continues. Each time she drops the stick, the male retrieves it. Each time she flies a little lower, a little faster and with a bigger stick. If the male ever fails to catch the falling stick, the female will chase him off and will not play anymore. The game climaxes when the female is flying at a tremendous speed in a nipand-tuck figure eight, less than 500 feet from the ground releasing an object weighing almost as much as she weighs expecting the male to nab the log without crashing into the ground (he almost has to be an olympic star). After finally satisfying the female that he is a fit husband, the eagles make their vows to one another.

Line art of a male and female during marriage vows.

The marriage vows of the eagles are made at an altitude between ten and fifteen thousand feet. It is done by locking talons together (feet to feet) and turning head-over-heels. This monumental moment in the eagle's life is also enhanced with both birds screaming at each other in joy.

After having made these vows, the eagles will remain together for life; for richer or poorer, in sickness and in health, till death do them part. They will hunt together, nest together, raise young together and, if need be, migrate together (the eagle is not normally a migrating bird).

As I write this chapter, there is an almost overwhelming desire to do a spiritual interpretation of this part of the eagle's life. However, without trying to write a mystery I must, for the sake of organization, withhold the spiritual analogy until chapter nine.

5
Eagle Homemakers

Once the eagles have made their vows and completed the ceremonies, they begin at once to build a home together. The first matter is to decide on a location which, to the eagles, is one of the most important decisions they will ever make. The average eagle will spend approximately fifty years in this location bearing young and reigning over their domain. Specifically, the eagles are instinctively looking for a high, inaccessible location with their backs turned to a rock wall.

"Does the eagle mount up ... and make his nest on a high [inaccessible place]? On the cliff he dwells ... upon the point of the rock." Job 39:27-29

The eagles may travel many miles together in search of just the right place. Finally, after much consideration, they decide on a location some 10,000 feet up in the crack of two large formations. The perfect spot. Now begins the painstaking job of building the massive nest which will, when completed, weigh between one and two tons. They must start adding to the rock formation limbs which will be strong enough to sustain the weight of the nest. Unfotunately, there are not any such materials readily available at the home site. The eagles must now fly down to ground level and procure the necessary branches. In the days and weeks to come, the eagles will make thousands of trips up and down carrying an almost unbelievable amount of building materials. They may at times even carry more than their own weight to an altitude of 10,000 feet. Once the major frame work is done, the female leaves the toting up to the male while she stays with the nest arranging and rearranging until the nest becomes a virtual fortress in the rocks. The nest is extremely deep with a shallow eighteen inch brooding area on top. The diameter of the nest will vary between six to ten feet, depending on the wing span of the eagles.

It will be composed of many things when completed. The frame, which is made of wood so that it will last for many years, may be four inch diameter limbs up to eight feet long. Building on up, the logs will get smaller in diameter until they are finally ready to put on the final cabinet work. The limbs have reduced in size now to one inch diameters, preferably green to allow some flexibility in positioning.

Now the finishing touches of the nest will include vines, which may be used to weave the upper layers together; leaves, which begin to add the soft home effect, and perhaps the fur of some recently devoured dinner, to make the home warm and soft enough for baby eagles.

In extreme contrast to the eagle, the vulture is not a committed spouse. The male will offer no help in locating or building a nest. The responsibility rests soley on the female, who may or may not give a hoot (a figure of speech, vultures do not literally hoot). Vultures would rather eat than nest, and so the housebuilding continues to be put off until one day the female realizes it is too late. Frantically she seeks out an old tree, perhaps a fallen log or if worse comes to worse, a grassy field, to lay her eggs. (They are not likely to receive the Mother of the Year award).

Of course the spiritual and moral implications of this chapter should be more than obvious. It is not hard to see the parallels between the Christian marriage and the eagles', or even the 'noncommital' marriage of the world and the vultures', but let me take just a few minutes to point out some of the less obvious analogies.

The fact that the eagles build their nest high in the mountain is a clear sign of God's dealing with men on the mountain. It was on Mount Moriah that God called Abraham to sacrifice Issac. It later became Mount Zion, and the location of the temple. It was on the thundering Mount Sinai that God told Moses to remove his sandals and later delivered the Ten Commandments. Joshua built an altar to the Lord on Mount Ebal. God assembled the prophets of Baal along with Elijah, on Mount Carmel. Jesus preached, prayed and was tempted on the mountain. He was transfigured on a mountain and He died on a mountain. Yes, we indeed have a high calling from God. Phillippians 3:14 says:

> "I press on toward the goal to win the [supreme and heavenly] prize to which God in Christ Jesus is **calling us upward**."

Here we see the deep commitment of the male eagle as he brings in the nesting materials for the female to arrange. Notice the wing span which will vary between 6 to 10 feet. *Photo: G. Wolf*

And in the book of Hebrews, chapter three and verse one, God calls us with the same calling of the eagle, a heavenly calling:

"So then brethren, consecrated and set apart for God, who share in the **heavenly calling** thoughtfully and attentively consider Jesus . . ."

A true sign of the Eagle Christian is that he has an inner unction to get higher, closer to God and to live in the heavenly places with Christ. The Eagle Christian makes his home there. He will not be satisfied to build his home in a tree or bear his young on the ground, but searches carefully for the cleft of the rock and there will live out his life in safety.

Perhaps this insight into the nature of the eagle will give you some new insight to a favored Bible chapter. Read it carefully, this chapter applies only to the Eagle Christian.

"He who dwells in the **secret place** of the **Most High** shall remain **stable** and **fixed** under the shadow of the Almighty (whose power no foe can withstand). I will say of the Lord, **He is my refuge** and **my fortress**, my God, on Him I lean and rely, and in Him I (confidently) trust! For then He will deliver you from the snare of the fowler and from the deadly pestilence. [Then] He will **cover you with His pinions** and **under His wings** shall you trust and find refuge; His truth and faithfulness are a shield and a buckler. [Then] You shall not be afraid of the terror of the night, nor of the arrow [the evil plots and slander of the wicked] that flies by day, Nor of the pestilence that stalks in darkness, nor of the destruction and sudden death that surprise and lay waste at noonday. [Then] A thousand may fall at your side and ten thousand at your right hand, but **it shall not come near you. Only a spectator shall you be [yourself inaccessible in the secret place of the Most High]** as you witness the reward of the wicked. Because **you have made the Lord your refuge and the Most High your dwelling place**, There shall no evil befall you nor any plague come near your tent." Psalm 91:1-10

Photo: G. Wolf

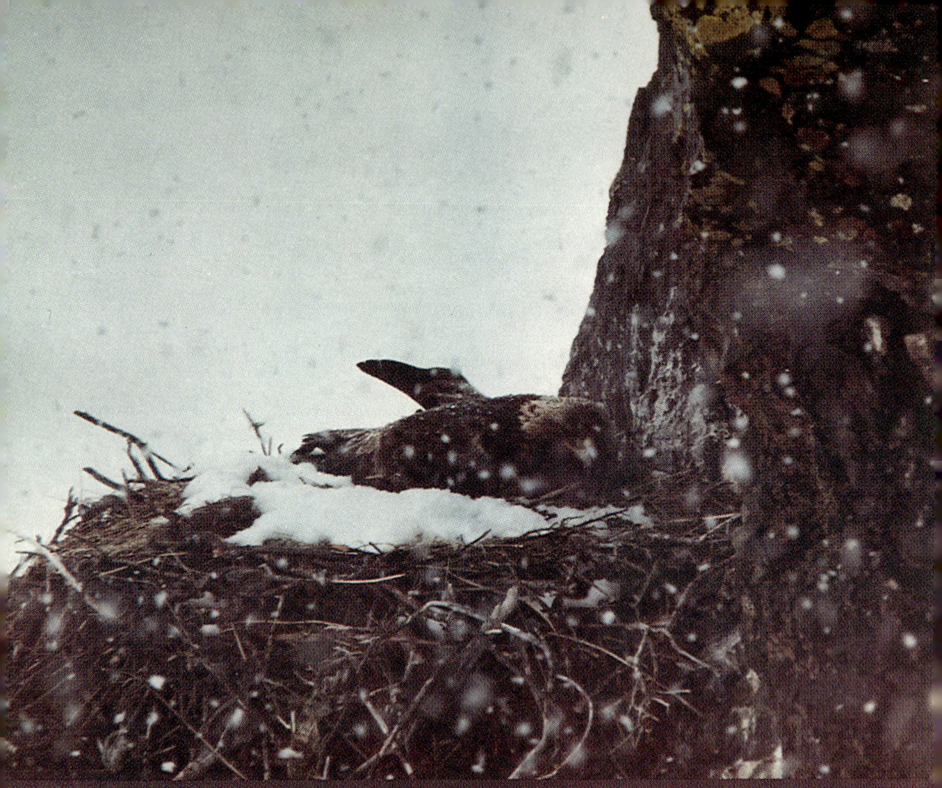

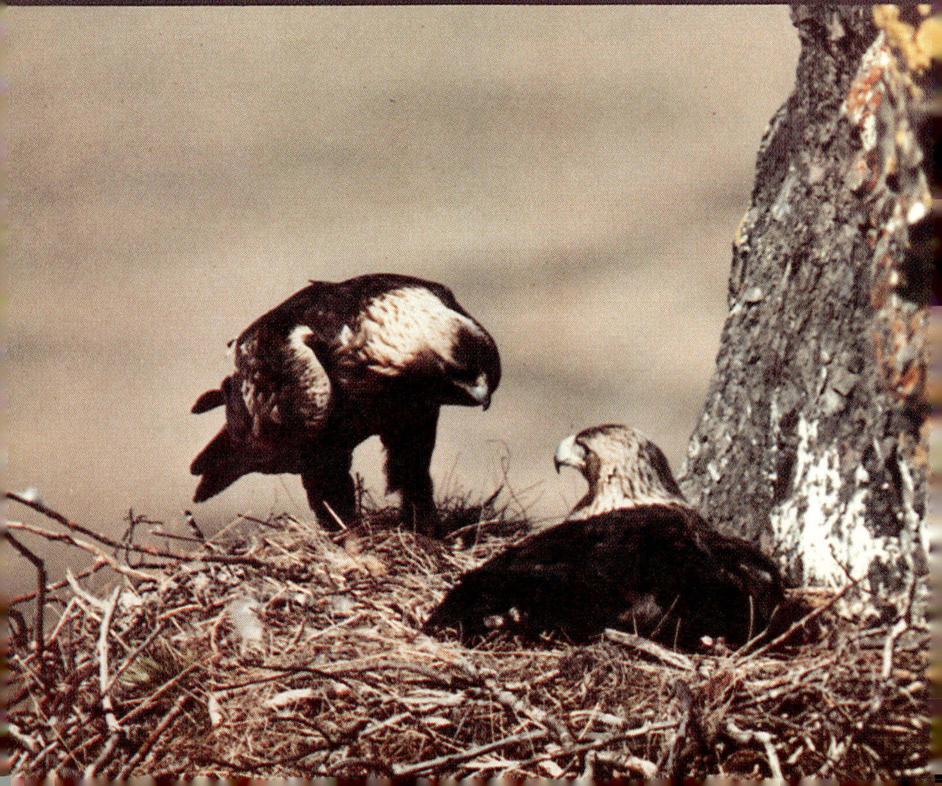

6
Lovingkindness of the Eagle

After painstakingly building their nest, the eagles are now ready to start their first family. Although there is still snow on the ground the eagle lays her eggs. She must remain at the nest until the snows are melted in order to keep the eggs warm during incubation. The sole responsibility of food now rests on the male who will in the next few months spend all his time hunting and fishing to feed the family. This is not an easy task when the snow is still on the ground because much of the food supply has disappeared during the winter months. The beauty of this part of the eagle's life is not found in many other birds. The eagles have not flown south for the winter (for reasons which will be discussed later) but instead they have endured the winter months. The eagle and the Eagle Christian are creatures of faith who do not run away during the cold months; they remain and lay their eggs of intercession, believing that spring will come again and life will return. It is a lonely time in the life of the Christian when it seems that everyone has gone. The revival fires of summer have passed and many of those who filled the sanctuary have long since disappeared. Perhaps the Eagle Christian wonders if he should remain alone or follow the flocks of others who have gone where the hunting is easier. Haven't we seen those times of revival when the sanctuaries were full of zealous, well-meaning people turn into a handful of remaining souls who go before God in prayer and cry, "God of grace, send us the fires of revival?" The Eagle Christian is not easily discouraged by the winter of the church nor the lifestyle of others because he does not direct his life by what is easiest or what is popular.

The mother eagle normally lays one to three eggs. However, she will not raise more than two eaglets. As the time approaches for the

Top: A female eagle brooding her eggs in the snow. Below: An expectant father sits anxiously by (the baby eagles hatched the following day). *Photos: G. Wolf.*

eggs to hatch. the mother eagle will begin to pull from her breast a downy fur to prepare a soft and warm bedding for the eaglets. This gives the eaglets the feeling of being surrounded by their mother. Everything is waiting for the new life to spring forth. Perhaps you are wondering what father eagle has been doing all this time. Well, he has been serving mother eagle breakfast in bed for several weeks. (This really helps to hold the marriage together). However, in his spare time he has become a doting father rounding up all kinds of things for the eaglets to amuse themselves: a shoe, a golf ball. an empty can or just anything that he takes a fancy to. Mother eagle is a little more practical and will dispose of many of the things that dad has brought home (Somebody has got to keep house). The unsuspecting reader would perhaps read right through this and be a little amused and miss one of the greatest revelations of the nature of God. We are quick to quote those Scriptures that relate to God's protection over us yet we so often fail to see the lovingkindness of the Lord. "Because Your lovingkindness is better than life . . ." (Psalms 63:3). Hasn't He, as a father eagle, brought into our lives those things which bring us pleasure? Perhaps the beauty of the flowers, or the majesty of the mountains or the sea, rainbows, butterflies, and the fragrance of the rose, which all serve about as much purpose to us as a golf ball does to the eaglet. And note too, the tender love and sacrifice of the mother eagle as she pulls the downy fur from her breast for the comfort of her young and maintains a constant watch over the eaglets. This is the perfect portrait of Jesus, who left His heavenly home to come and live among us, sacrificed His life, and who, upon returning to heaven, said to us, "Lo, I am with you always even unto the end of the earth." He keeps watch over us with an eagle's eye.

Photos of mother eagle pulling off small pieces of food to satisfy the cries of her young. *Photo: G. Wolf*

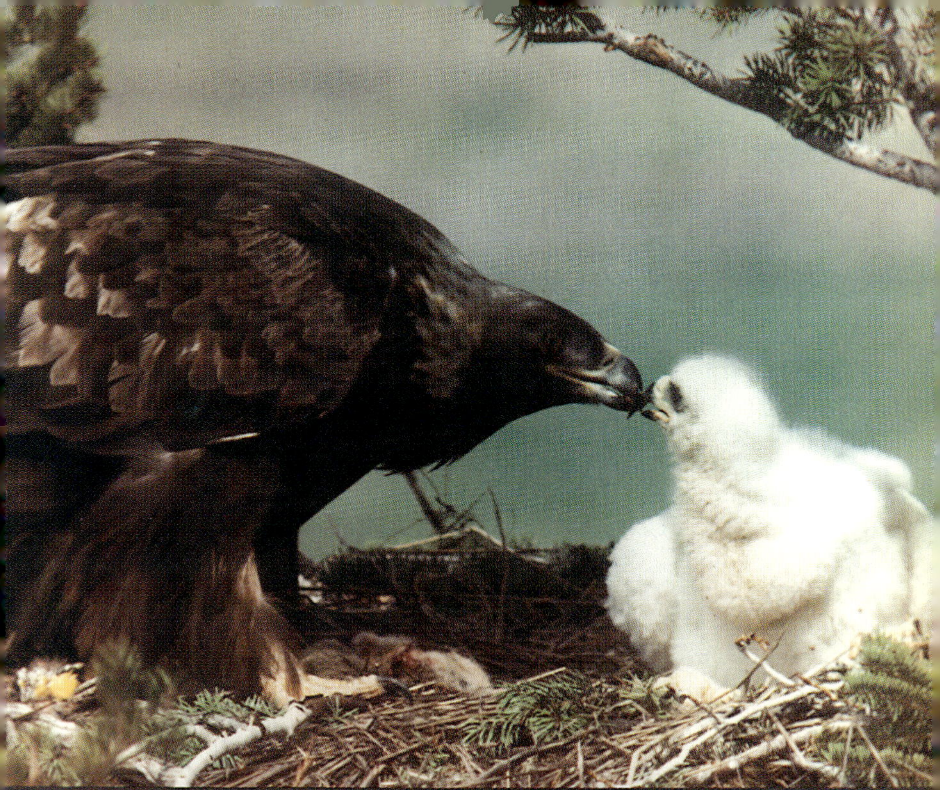
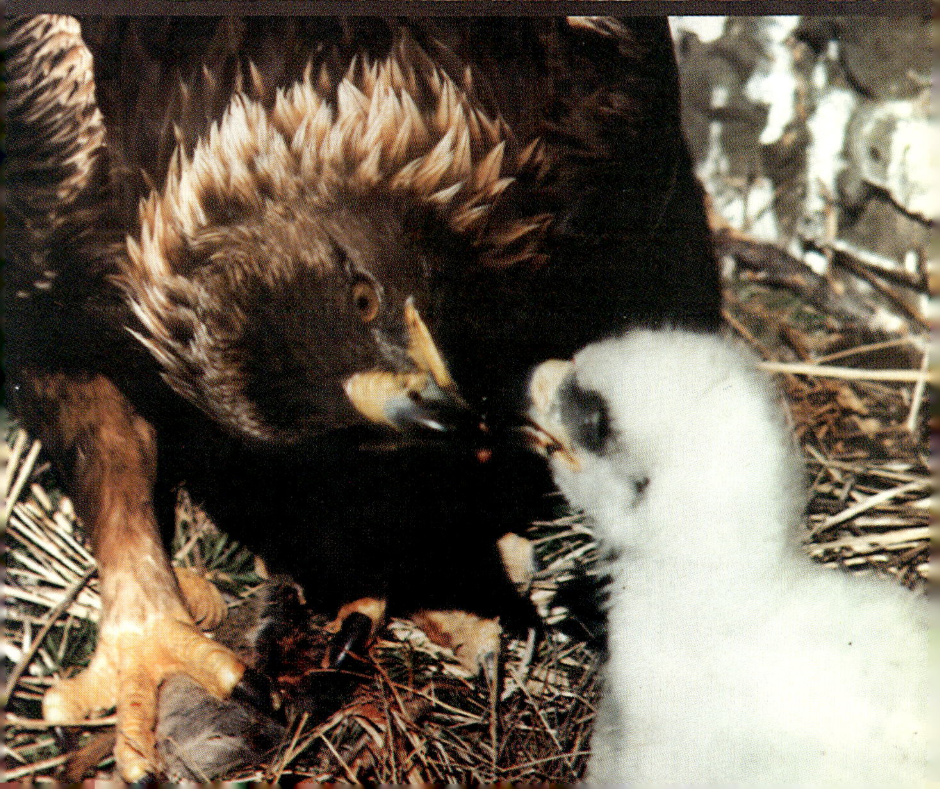

7
Eagle Elementary

Soon after the eaglets hatch they begin a cry that will last for several weeks. It is a constant cry for food and soon it will require the skill of both parents to meet the great demand for food. They must hunt from sunup to sundown in order to keep the eaglets, as well as themselves, satisfied and nourished. As the eaglets grow so do their appetites, but the parents faithfully provide. Life in the nest is truly a life of leisure - nothing to do but eat and sleep. Everything has been provided for the comfort and safety of the eaglets. Because of the quality and quantity of food the eaglets get, they mature at a much faster rate than other birds their size (twice as fast as vultures).

As the eaglets grow stonger, mother knows it is time for school to begin. A most unfortunate ordeal for man and eagle alike. However, eaglehood is not attained by lying comfortably on the downy padding nor sitting on the church pew. Before this time it seemed that comfort and ease would never end, but mother and dad knew that the eaglets would soon have to be able to provide for themselves (pay the taxes and the light bill, not to mention grocery shopping). And on one beautiful spring day mom comes gliding into the nest. But this time she has a wild look in her eye. She jumps down into the brooding area and begins to squawk. The eaglets have never seen mom like this before. She stomps around picking up the toys and hurling them over the edge piece by piece. The eaglets are just trying to stay out of mom's way. Now with all the toys gone the eaglets figure it will settle down a bit, but mom isn't through yet. She takes the rabbit fur pillow and slings it over the side then she uses her great wings to sweep house. Down goes the downy fur that has kept the eaglets warm and protected all these weeks. They can no longer just lie around because the sticks will poke them in the breast. They must now use their own talons (feet) to hold themselves up. After thoroughly cleaning house mom takes flight to procure food. The eaglets are just thankful she is gone and they convince themselves she will come back in a better mood.

It is not easy for the eaglets to balance themselves on the remaining sticks but the alternative is not very pleasant either. However, each day their talons grow stonger and their sense of balance, too. The lesson mom has taught here has begun preparing

24

the eaglets to catch their own food. Only strong talons could hold a wiggling fish or rabbit while returning to the nest.

And so it is with the Eaglet Christian for whom, after falling in love with the comfort and ease of being a baby Christian, school begins. We go from one church meeting to the next soaking up the food, rushing to Sunday school and Bible study, spending hours in the "Religion" section of the bookstore, only to find that the Holy Spirit has decided to clean house. His objective is to prepare us for the real world where hurt and pain and endurance are a way of life. Without the proper training an Eaglet Christian would surely fall. Remember those early days when you would no sooner cry out to God than He would answer, but now God is more concerned with your maturity than with your comfort. Education often comes by "comfort removal."

The eaglet is not aware of the value of what he is learning; he only knows it is hard. So we, too, seldom understand the value of our education until the education is well over. We may feel as though God has forsaken us and no longer cares about us. We may feel that God no longer cares about our comfort but nothing could be farther from the truth. This temporary inconvenience will point out some weakness in our life and serve as an exercise to strengthen that area, so that we may have the strength in that area.

"Although He was a Son, He learned obedience through what He suffered." Hebrews 5:8

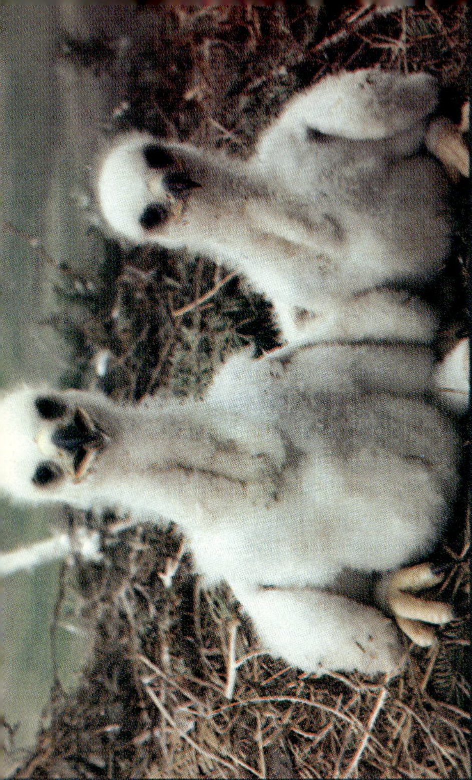
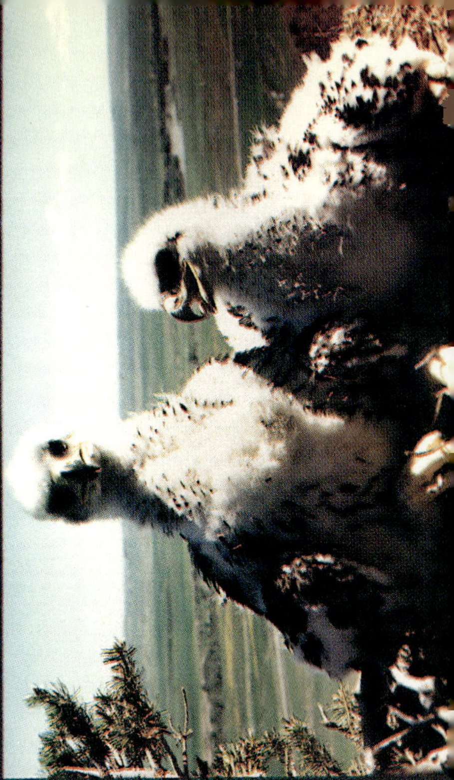
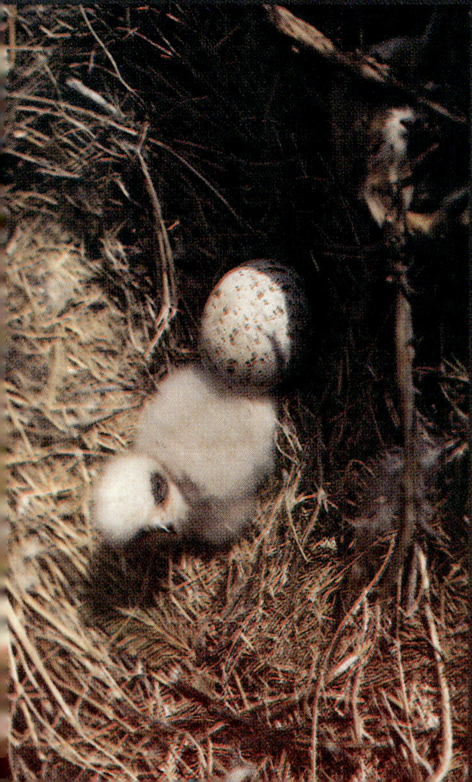
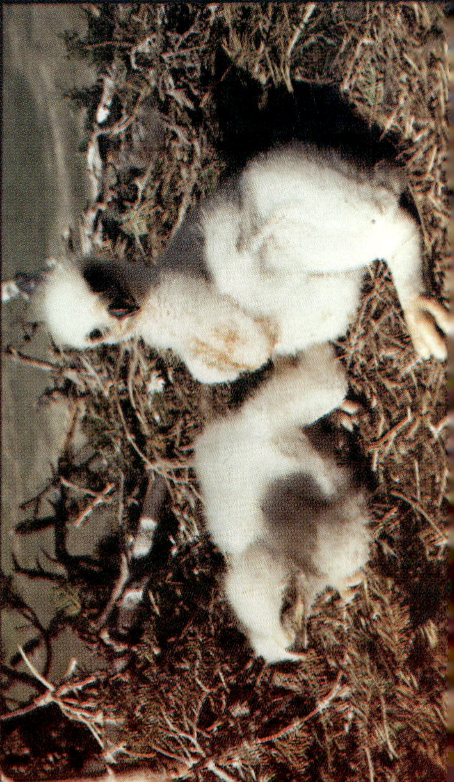

8
The Ugly Eaglet

As you can tell from the photographs in this chapter, the eaglet, almost from the time of birth, is an unusually cumbersome and unattractive creature. The soft white down on the eaglet at birth is accented by the racoon-type eyes which are covered with black down which makes them appear as though they have black eyes. Not to mention the awkward wings, feet and legs which are so far out of proportion with the rest of the little creature.

You may also notice some size difference in the two eaglets. There will, as a rule, be one eaglet larger than the other. This is due to the difference of the time of birth which is usually 24 hours apart. The larger eagle is actually a day older and simply starts eating sooner than the other. This difference which is so obvious during early development, will not begin to disappear until the post-fledgling period (approximately 6 to 10 weeks), but will be completely unnoticable by the time the eaglets reach the juvenile stage (approximately 11 months). At which time it will be quite difficult to tell them apart by size alone unless they are male and female.

The post-fledgling period of the eagle's life is the climax of ugliness. During this time he will lose his downy white fur in exchange for some short brown feather freckles, a process that would humble the proudest peacock. But then we are not seeing the young through the eyes of the parents. The old saying, "A face only a mother could love" would be quite appropriate for the eaglet at this stage of development.

The ugliness will remain with the eaglet until approximately the time of his first hunting expedition. By this time the down is completely gone and the feather freckles have become sturdy feathers. However, there is still one main visual difference between the young eaglet and his parents, and that is the golden crown on his parents' heads.

You can observe in some of the photographs in this book that the parent eagles have a golden crown which covers the entire head and neck much like the white crown on the bald eagle. This crown is a fairly good gauge of the eagle's age. Each time the eagle molts (a process in which the feathers are replaced) the crown grows a little

The photos here from left to right are a stage-by-stage development of two eaglets. *Photos: G. Wolf*

darker and a little larger until it becomes the most outstanding feature of the golden eagle. This family of eagles is not named by the color of its body but rather by the markings on the head -- thus we have the golden eagle.

This story has striking similarities with the story of "The Ugly Duckling," but it also very closely parallels the maturing process of a young Christian. Although he is quite safe and secure, even hidden from the world, there is still much in the life of a young Christian that is unattractive. As the caterpillar changes into a butterfly and the down of the eaglet into feathers so too must the young Christian give up his former infancy to become an Eagle Christian. It is an awkward thing to try and use 'faith' as a young Christian, about as awkward as the oversized feet of the eaglet who has a tool but not the knowledge to use it. Many of the gifts and blessings of God are there in the life of the young Christian, but it may be some time before those wings of faith become effective tools. This is a time of separation from the world because you just don't fit in (kind of like the ugly duckling). One may be mocked and scorned for this strange new life but no one scorns a matured eagle, for he possesses what all others desire.

The unique growing process of the two eagles and the size difference between them is a picturesque example of how this maturing process takes place in the life of a Christian. The speed at which young Christians grow varies from one to another. I have seen some almost shoot up overnight while others seem to take a good bit more time, but the end result was always the same; a usable vessel for the Lord. Eaglet Christians should avoid comparing their growth to others their same age. Instead they should apply themselves to becoming what they can be and attain the golden crown of maturity.

Much could be said for the crown that is given to the golden eagle when compared to the crowns awarded to the mature Eagle Christian. The Scripture speaks of grey hair as a crown of wisdom. Like the eagle's crown, those grey hairs of wisdom are the result of slow but blessed changes that seem to lift us up to higher planes of understanding, compassion and Godly insight.

The Bible speaks of many different crowns but all crowns are the reward of victory given to one who endures. Each hardship, each difficulty is another step closer to the crown of life which is promised to those who endure.

Notice here the great contrast between parents and young. The young will one day possess the crown of maturity themselves. Photo: G. Wolf

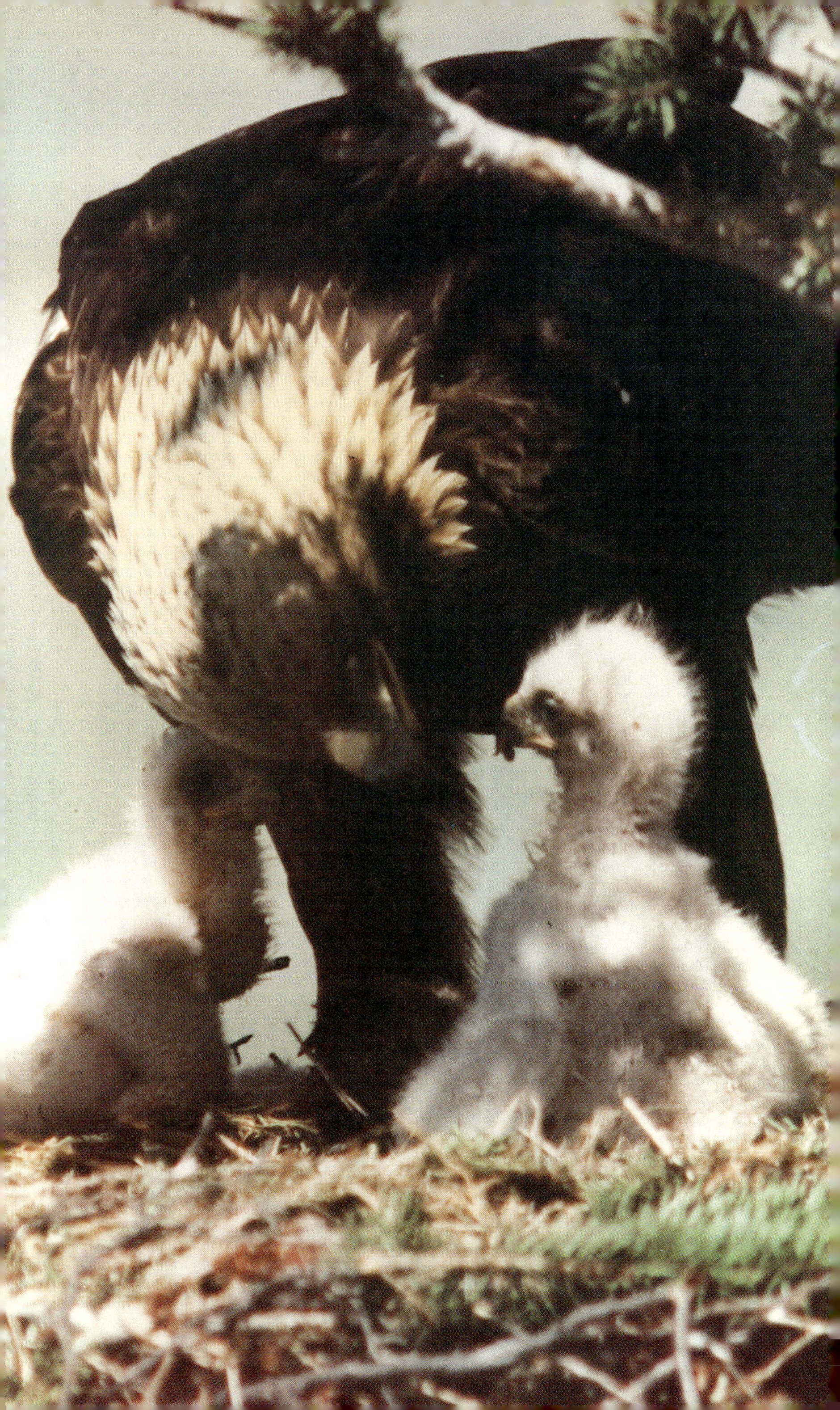

"Blessed, happy, to be envied is the man who is patient under trial and stands up under temptation, for when he has stood the test and been approved he will receive (the victor's) **crown of life** which God has promised to those who love Him." James 1:12

In the same way that the eagles are named by the color of the head (the Golden Eagle) we as members of God's family are named and crowned in His likeness. Christ is the head and so we are called Christians.

"The twenty-four elders (the members of the heavenly Sanhedrin) fall prostrate before Him Who is sitting on the throne and they worship Him Who lives forever and ever; and **they throw down their crowns before the throne**, crying out, Worthy are You, our Lord and God, to receive the glory and the honor and dominion, for You created all things; by Your will they were (brought into being) and were created." Revelation 4:10-11

As the eaglet matures he begins to resemble his parents more and more and so it is with the Eaglet Christian.

"And all of us...are constantly being **transfigured into his** very **own** image in ever increasing **splendor and from one degree of glory to another; [for this comes] from the Lord [Who is] the Spirit**." II Corinthians 3:18

9
Eagle University

Now as the eaglets have learned to support their already massive bodies, they will frequently watch as their parents soar high above the nest and especially when they see them flying in from a distance with food. They marvel at the skill and ability of their parents. And then without any further warning comes the most dreadful day that has ever come to the eaglets. Time has caused them to forget mother's cruel disposal of their toys and bedding, but mom has again come home with a very wild look in her eyes. Instead of sitting on the side of the nest she jumps down into the brooding area and begins to flutter her wings. The eaglets scream, hoping dad will come and stop this insanity, but he continues to fly high above the nest as though nothing is happening. Soon mother begins to nudge one of the eaglets closer and closer to the edge of the nest until baby eaglet is looking over the edge some ten thousand feet below. A very strange sensation comes over the eaglet as he sees the ground below. It is a sense of death; a frightening experience. He is astonished by what appears to be the cruelty of his mother. And then in all of mother's shuffling around, baby eaglet is thrown over.

"As an **eagle** that **stirs up her nest**, that flutters over her young, He spread abroad His wings; He took them, **He bore them on His pinions**." Deuteronomy 32:11

Now the sense of death is more real. Little eaglet, now falling from the nest, is sure that his mother is insane. As he is falling some ten thousand feet, an instinct takes over -- the instinct to live. He screams for help and begins to imitate his parents. He flaps his young and clumsy wings until he is so weak he can no longer flap. He is now only a few thousand feet from certain death when suddenly he catches a glimpse of father eagle, who swoops up under baby eaglet just before he crashes into the ground below. With lightning speed, father eagle has correctly calculated the last possible moment to save eaglet and has executed his job with perfection.

You can now see the importance of the dating game (chapter 3) in the life of the eagles. Each must be precision pilots if they are to raise their young. Father eagle returns the eaglet to the nest and prepares for lesson number two. What, to the eaglet, seems to be the most cruel thing his parents could do will turn out to be the most beneficial thing he will learn from them, and that is how to fly. They are teaching the eaglets to be eagles.

Understanding this part of the eagle's life sheds a great deal of light on the courtship of the eagles who have performed this same stunt hundreds of times with sticks (chapter 3).

We should take time here to evaluate every morsel of truth as it pertains to the Eagle Christian. First of all, we should notice that before the eaglet is taught how to fly he is taught how to stand. What value is it to fly if your feet are not able to uphold you when you get there? And so it is with the Christian. We must throw off the cushion of our spiritual crib and learn to walk. Certainly we will fall but eventually we will not only walk but run, not only run but we shall run and not be weary. This preparation in the Eagle Christian's life is done by having our feet shod with the preparation of the Gospel (Ephesians 6). If we only shod our feet with, "For God so loved the world. . ." we will not have strength to stand. We must also prepare ourselves with "love your enemies," "go and sell all that you have," "take up your cross and follow me." It is this kind of preparation that will allow us to have our feet firmly planted when the time arises.

Once the Eagle Christian has mastered standing, he will begin to marvel at the majesty of God, making spiritual note of His accuracy, swiftness, fearlessness, dominion, authority and freedom. Having once seen these things, the Christian determines to pay whatever price to attain them. We, like the eaglets, will marvel at the skill and abilities of our Father. Once the decision to pay the price is made, God sets the course of our life for "Eaglehood."

It starts without any warning. We find ourselves being nudged to the edge with no way to escape. We sense, like the eaglet, a helplessness and a sense of death. We wonder why we are treated like this and then it happens -- we find ourselves in a situation where everything is at stake, perhaps our home, our family, our job, our health or maybe all of them and down we go. Like the eaglet we scream out to God, we flap our spiritual wings, we grab at every limb and in all of our efforts, we become weak and learn to trust God in whatever peril we are facing. And then as though it were all planned, with lightning speed, our Father comes and bears us up on His wings and delivers us from the peril.

A thousand questions race through our minds. First, "God, why did you let this happen?" He replies, "You can't learn to fly in a church pew and you can't soar on the preacher's back." "Okay, why

These two eaglets are about the age for their first flight lesson. The larger one is a female. *Photo: G. Wolf*

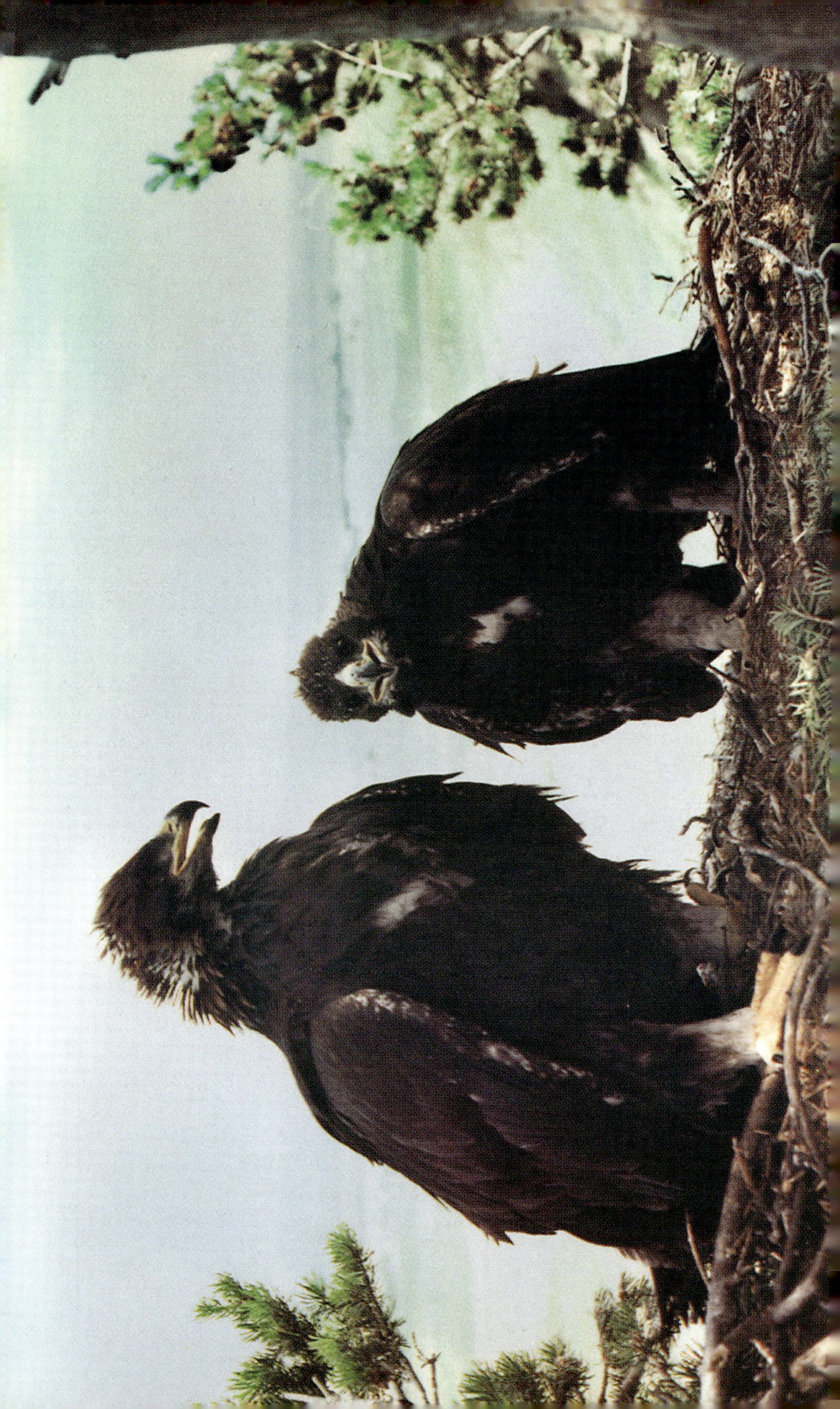

did you wait so long to catch me?" He replies, "You needed all the time you could get to learn to fly." With those things in mind He returns us to the nest and prepares us for lesson two. And we overcome the greatest obstacle of flying -- fear. He is the God of the twelfth hour and although He may take His own sweet time, He will not be late for class, nor will he miss a single flying lesson.

In the lessons that follow, the eaglet and the Eagle Christian will learn many things about flying and will be well on their way to eaglehood. All the kicking and screaming will soon stop, the fear of smashing into the ground will disappear and the eaglet will be free to become an eagle.

> "Bless the Lord, O my soul, and all that is within me, bless His holy name! Bless the Lord, O my soul, and forget not all His benefits, who forgives all your iniquities, Who heals all your diseases; **Who redeems your life** from the pit and corruption; **Who beautifies, dignifies and crowns you** with loving-kindness and tender mercies; **Who satisfies your mouth** with good; so that your youth, renewed, is **like the eagle's**." Psalms 103:1-5

> "You have seen what I did to the Egyptians, and **how I bore you on eagles' wings and brought you to myself**." Exodus 19:4

This is the lift-off pattern of a mature eagle. Notice how he mounts the wind.

10
The Preying Eagle

The hunting abilities of the eagles actually start during the juvenile period of their lives. This is between one and four years old. It is a time of trial and error in developing their flying, stalking and capturing abilities. It is the inevitable time of training that seems to be a part of every animal's life. During this time in the eagle's life he lives alone, away from his parents. He is not yet ready for marriage vows as he is not skilled enough to provide for a family, so he spends this time learning.

Flying has now become easy in comparision to the way he used to struggle just to stay up. But flying and preying are two completely different things. A flying eagle drifts and soars with the wind currents. Unfortunately, he can't always wait to find dinner downwind. He must learn to fly against the wind. He must learn to dive bomb (a process in which he simply folds in his wings and allows gravity to pull him down). During this particular tactic the eagle may attain a speed of two hundred miles per hour (that's almost four times the speed limit on our highways). Needless to say, this type of attack takes practice. Not so much how to dive bomb but more importantly, how to pull out in time.

All the eagle has to rely on is the memory of his parents who were skilled hunters. It will be some time before he becomes as proficient as his parents. Once the tactics have been learned, the eagle will be able to obtain almost any prey he chooses.

Because the wings and feathers are the eagle's primary means of obtaining food, each morning the eagle will spend at least an hour preening his feathers. Preening is a process in which each feather is passed through the beak simultaneously with exhaled air. This is a type of steam cleaning. This also seals the individual hairs of the feathers together much like a zip lock. Through the course of the day these feathers will be beaten and will take much abuse from the wind during the maneuvering of the skilled eagle. The outer

These four photos are all part of the hunting process: the eagle spies his prey, assumes a mounting position and closes in for the catch.
Photo: G. Wolf

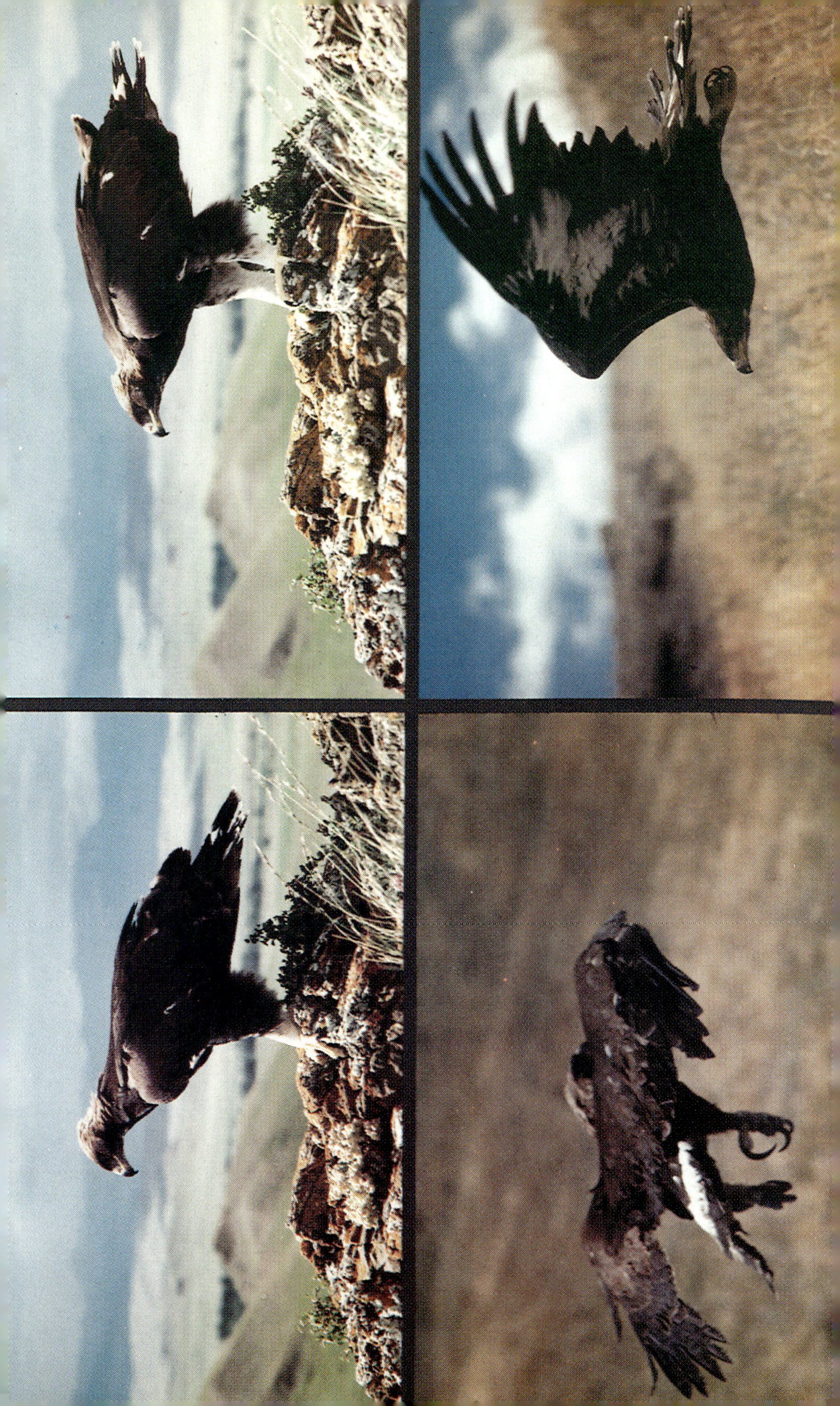

feathers will not only be steam-cleaned, they will also be waterproofed by a chemical secreted by the "preening gland." This is extremely necessary if the eagle is to capture fish or prey on some other animal in the water.

Once the preening is done the eagle will sit on the side of the nest and observe his territory. During this time he may spy out his first meal for the day. If so, he will mount the wind and begin circling round and round high above the prey. This circling allows him ample time to get a feel of the wind currents in order to calculate his speed and direction of attack. There is also great thought put into the size of the prey so that the eagle does not get anything so large that he cannot carry it.

"On the cleft he dwells... from there he spies out the prey..." Job 39:27-29

The analogies in this chapter are probably the least obvious of all. Nevertheless, they are there. In keeping with the train of thought that the Word of God is the diet of Eagle Christians, we will be able to see how these analogies apply to our own lives.

The time of learning is that time when we, like the juvenile eagle, must learn how to obtain food for ourselves. (I think here of the great men of God who were called out into the wilderness to be taught of God before beginning their ministry). This training period will sharpen our lives so that we can continue on into our calling. Diving is the most dangerous flight tactic of the eagle and is a good example of faith to the Eagle Christian. It involves the powerful force of gravity and the aerodynamics of parachuting. The analogy here is that the power of God is a force (like gravity) available for use by the trained Christian. The eagle, in all of his strength, could not attain this kind of speed without the use of gravity. And so, the Eagle Christian cannot do, in his own strength, the works of God. Rather, he must learn to operate in the realm of the spirit.

The preening of the eagle should be a good lesson in holiness to the Eagle Christian. In the same way that the eagle starts his day cleaning and preparing himself for the day's work, the Eagle Christian must also prepare himself. Removing all uncleanliness and preparing for battle should be a daily process for the Eagle Christian. The observation of the eagle from his nest is a clear example of how each day has purpose to the Eagle Christian, purpose with direction. Until we receive flight instructions for the day, we are not yet ready to leave the nest. The examination of the prey, the feel of the wind, the calculations for attack are all symbolic of the great care that the skilled Eagle Christian puts into his feeding, not only for himself but also for his young.

"Saul, and Jonathan beloved and lovely! In their lives and in their death they were not divided; **they were swifter than eagles,** they were stronger than lions." II Samuel 1:23

11
Eagle Eye

Like most animals, the eaglets' eyes are not fully developed when they first hatch. They will not be able to focus for several weeks. However, there is a very unique property of the eagles' eyes which, when understood, will offer a great deal of light to the Christian. Inside the eagles' eyes are a series of tissues folded into pleats which are called pectens. Each pleat contains a fine network of lymph tubes. The lymph fluid in these tubes is electrolyte. That means it is affected by magnetic pull and operates as a conductor of electricity. When the eagle is young and the eyes are not fully developed, these tubes are pliable. They are affected by the magnetic pull of the North Pole very similar to a compass. The pectens adjust themselves to the lines of magnetic intensity from the North Pole in relation to their place of birth. As the eaglet matures over the next few months, these pectens become more rigid and by the time the eaglet reaches maturity they are permanently set. As long as the eagle is away from his nesting ground there is a sense of imbalance. These pectens are acting as a built-in gyroscope for the eagle. There is a constant pressure in the eagle's eyes which cause pain, to some degree, during times of migration. However, the pain subsides as the eagle returns to his nesting ground. It is not difficult for the eagle to find his way home even from thousands of miles away because God has equipped him with an infallible sense of direction.

The Eagle Christian in his youth is much like the eaglet, unable to focus on things clearly. Paul wrote, "We see through a glass dimly." However, his sense of sight will improve as he matures. In the same way that God has placed this mysterious force in the eagle's life that causes him to always seek his home ground, God has also placed the desire in man to seek a place of rest. Like the eagle's pectens, set on an immovable North Pole, the Eagle Christian's eyes are set on an immovable God. From any point in the universe, man can at anytime find his way to God. This truth is borne out by the scripture in Proverbs 22:6, "Train up a child in the way he should go and when he is old, he will not depart from it."

As I have seen men age, I have noticed a continuing sense of emptiness and uselessness come over them when they refuse to seek that place of rest that only God can give. It is as if they too were experiencing some kind of anguish for their homeland. But, "In the fear of the Lord is strong confidence; and His children shall have a place of refuge." Proverbs 14:26.

Another fascinating characteristic of the eagle's eyes is their ability to sharply focus on objects several miles away. This ability, coupled with the nesting and flying instincts of the eagle, give him a better than "birds'-eye-view." He is able to find his food quickly and identify impending danger. Likewise, the Eagle Christian has an uncanny ability to see things in the distance of time and discern them accurately. Not only is this characteristic of the Eagle Christian, it is characteristic of our heavenly Father. Ezra wrote,

> "The **eyes of the Lord run to and fro throughout the whole earth** to show himself strong in behalf of those whose heart is blameless toward him." II Chronicles 16:9

> "From there he spies out the prey, and **His eyes see it afar off.**" Job 39:29

The eagles' ability to separate colors and hues is several times greater than human ability and so it is with the Eagle Christian who is able to see more beauty and depth to life than the non-Christian.

One final point I would like to make about the eagles' eyes is that they are covered with two sets of eyelids. The first set of eyelids is used when in flight or for observation from the nest. The second set is used when flying directly into the sun, which would otherwise be blinding. Because of this second eyelid, the eagle is able to stare intently at the sun. This ability gives him a great advantage over other birds. This particular aspect brings to mind the inability of the non-Christian to see or even draw near to God. Only when shielded and protected by the blood of Jesus are men able to approach the Light.

> "But the natural, nonspiritual man does not accept or welcome or admit into his heart the gifts and teachings and revelations of the Spirit of God, for they are folly (meaningless nonsense) to him; and he is incapable of knowing them — of progressively recognizing, understanding and becoming better acquainted with them — because they are spiritually discerned and estimated and appreciated." I Corinthians 2:14

12

The Eagle's Enemy

Because of his nesting place, as well as his size, strength and swiftness in flight, the eagle has only one primary enemy which poses any great threat. Ironically, it is the same enemy of the spiritual man, the serpent. Almost from the beginning of time (which started at the fall of Adam, because everything before that was eternal) God put an instinctive hatred between man and the serpent.

> "And I will put enmity between you and the woman, and between your offspring and her offspring; He shall bruise and tread your head under foot and you will lie in wait and bruise His heel." Genesis 3:15

The mature eagle, however, is not so much threatened by the serpent as are the young eaglets before they learn to fly and use their beaks and talons. In the nest the eaglets are safely hidden from almost every other predator. However, the subtle snake will sliter up the cliff under the cover of the rocks and approach the nest in almost total silence. Most frequently he is discovered by the adult eagles before he gets close enough to do any harm to the young. However, should the serpent sneak up into the nest while the parents are away, he will attempt to devour either the eggs or the young. The eaglets, unaccustomed to anything moving except themselves, will begin to screech with all their might and alert mom to the fact that something is going on. The eaglet knows instinctively to allow his parents to handle this matter.

Mother eagle hears the cries of her young and with all swiftness returns prepared to do battle. Now there are two main ways the eagle has of dealing with the serpent. The first is to use her quick beak and peck the serpent to death. She may even lay hold of him with her talons and pull his head completely off. The other method is to lay hold of him and wing flight from the nest to remove all the danger away from the young ones. As she flies, snake grasped firmly, she uses her wide scope of vision to locate a large jagged rock on which she will drop the serpent, thereby crushing him.

We see in this photo the extreme caution of the mother eagle. She draws the young under wing and investigates any potential dangers.
Photo: G. Wolf

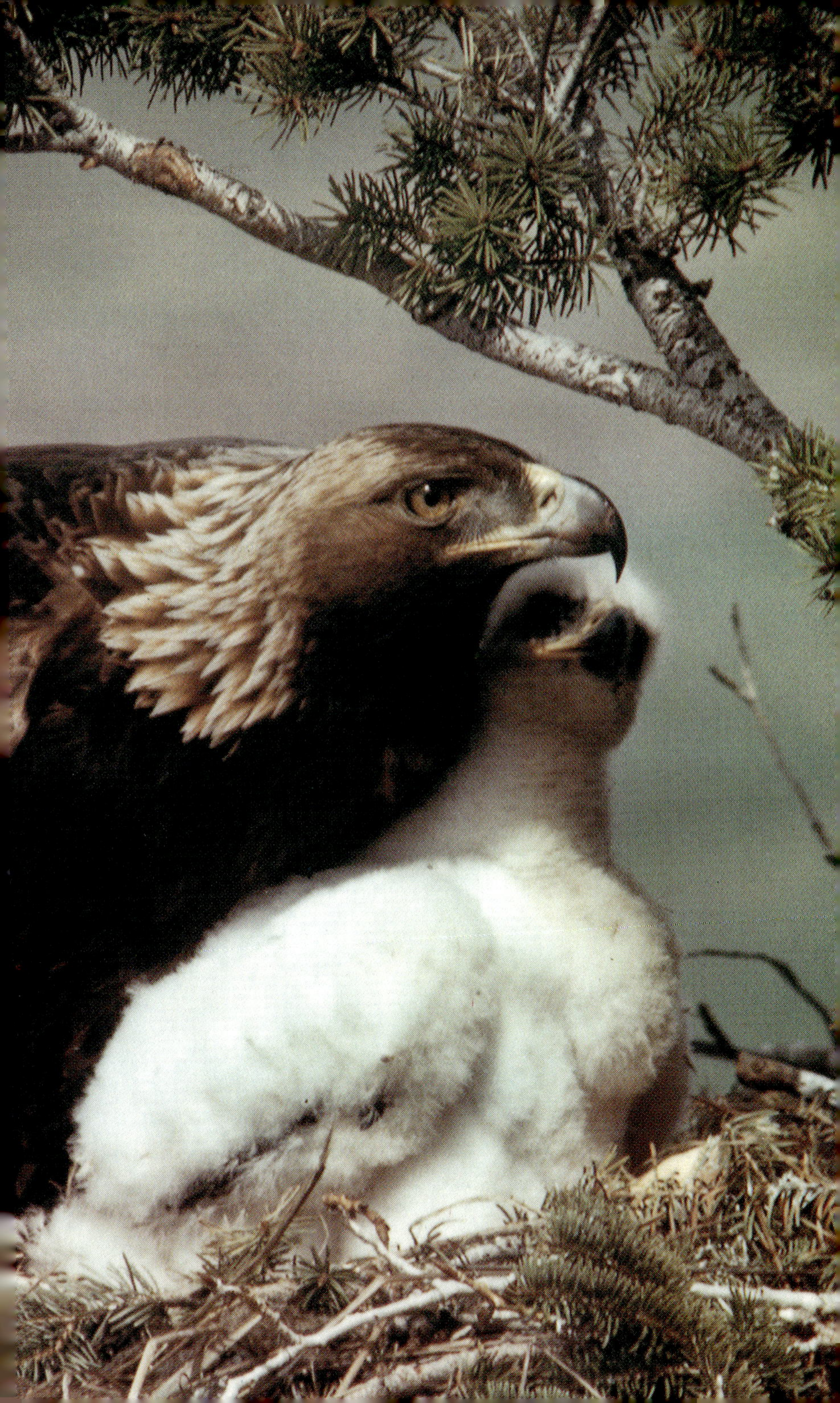

There are several lessons here for us to learn about the Eagle Christian. The first is the instinctive nature of the mature Christian to look out for and even do battle in behalf of the younger Christian. The second is the way the enemy (the devil) will slither up to the young and attack them when they are alone.

It has often been my observation that young Christians are more easily tempted when they have been separated from the rest of the flock. I have seen many devoured by the slyness of the devil simply because they did not have the maturity to fight and failed to call for help. It is not so much that help is not available but rather that it was not sought in time. Such is the case where two young Christians become sexually involved, not seeking counsel, and then discover that she is pregnant. At this point they run to their pastor or parents but the damage has been done, the bite of the serpent has left his scar on their lives.

The third analogy pertains to the swiftness of the mature eagles to come to the aid of the young. Only a mature Christian can see what is really at stake when the young are becoming the prey of the serpent. The keen vision of the Eagle Christian will usually allow him ample time to fight in behalf of the young against dangers they are not even aware of.

The last analogy revealed in this part of the eagle's life is the manner in which he deals with the serpent. If the eagle sees the serpent approaching, he attacks first. Many immature Christians stand around wringing their hands asking, "What are we going to do?" The Eagle Christian has no time for hand wringing when Satan invades his territory. The Eagle Christian is a conqueror and he rules over his domain.

> "Yet amid all these things **we are** more than **conquerors** and given a surpassing victory through Him who loved us." Romans 8:37

> "Behold! I have given you authority and **power to trample upon serpents** . . . and over all the power that the enemy [possesses] and nothing shall in any way harm you." Luke 10:19

Now notice the way in which the eagle fights and conquers the serpent. The pecking here is symbolic of the aggressive use of the Word of God against the very gates of hell. A clear example of "scriptural pecking" would be during Jesus' (the Master Eagle) temptation where He withstood Satan (the old snake) verbally with the Word of God (see Matthew 4:1-11). The second method, which is just as effective, was to drop him on a rock and allow the rock to rob the serpent of his power.

". . . and the Rock was Christ." I Corinthians 10:4

Even the Eagle CHristian finds it necessary to use a force and power greater than his own. Jesus is that force; Jesus is that power; Jesus is that Rock.

13
The Eagle in Sickness

The eagle is by nature an extremely healthy bird living as many as sixty years. It is not generally accustomed to sickness, due to its source of food. Unlike vultures, who will eat half decayed meat thereby raising their mortality rate, the eagle thrives mainly on living species which suggests that they are not eating diseased food. However, it is possible for an eagle to devour some creature and get "food poisoning." When this happens the eagle becomes weak. Although this is a serious problem it does not usually result in the death of the eagle. The eagle's instincts take over and he will locate some inaccessible place such as a cliff or butte and lie prostrate in the sunlight with his wings spread wide open. Once the eagle has done this he will fix his eyes firmly on the sun until the warmth of the sun and the natural body processes have returned his strength. Many who have observed the eagle in this position have assumed him to be dying, as this procedure occurs at three different times in the eagle's life — the first in sickness, the second when molting (shedding old feathers) and the third in death.

All three of these instances have the form of death and the eagle reacts to each one in the same way. However, in death the eagle will watch the sun go down and just as it is setting will close his eyes in death.

Sickness, the first of the three requires some real discernment to understand the analogy. From chapter three we discovered that the eagle's source of strength is his diet, the same is true of the Eagle Christian. If, however, the eagle were to eat some diseased food he would become sick and so it is with the Eagle Christian. It is quite possible that some untruth which looks good and smells good and certainly tastes good could get into the diet of the Eagle Christian. When this happens the Eagle Christian becomes ill. At this point he must allow his spiritual instincts to take over and prostrate himself before God and let His light of truth, His warmth of love do healing work as the Eagle Christian stares unchangingly at the Son. Like the eagle, this must be done in a place of solitude for the work to be safe and complete.

If the sickness is, in fact, the result of some part of the Eagle Christian's diet, he will learn not to eat that anymore. And so it has been in the Body of Christ for two thousand years. Diseased doctrine has infiltrated our species and given us "food poisoning." some of the greatest and strongest Eagle Christians have found themselves prostrate before God in search of spiritual truth. And God has responded with lovingkindness.

> "Who satisfies your mouth with good; so that **your youth renewed is like the eagles'** [strong, overcoming, soaring]!" Psalms 103:5

Secondly, the molting, although not due to "food poisoning," feels the same way and may be compared to those times in our lives in which God wants to put on us a new coat of His presence. The gleam of new feathers on the eagle is indeed a glorious sight and could be paralleled to the story of Moses after he came down from Mount Sinai (Exodus 34:29-35). Such is the glow of those who take their lives before God and allow him to change, renew and transform them.

> "And all of us, as with unveiled face continue to behold as in a mirror the glory of the Lord, are constantly being **transfigured into his very own image** in ever increasing splendor and from one degree of glory to another; [for this comes] from the Lord [Who is] the Spirit." II Corinthians 3:18

And finally the Eagle Christian will prostrate himself, fix his eyes on the Son of God and change from a body of humiliation to a glorified body as he closes his eyes in death.

> "... and the dead will be raised imperishable — free and immune from decay — and we shall be changed (transformed). For this perishable [part of us] must put on the imperishable [nature], and this mortal must put on immortality (freedom from death) ... **O death where is your victory ...**" I Corinthians 15:51-56

Death becomes the ultimate molting of the Eagle Christian as he is transformed into a more glorious body and is able to soar where no mortal eagle has ever soared — into the presence of his Creator.

14

The Lonely Eagle

No other bird nests where the eagle nests and after the first year (of fledgling) the eagle will not mate for at least three years until he becomes a skilled hunter and is capable of reproduction. He will live alone with no nest of his own. He will fly at altitudes where no other bird flies and observe the earth from afar. The eagle is not a gregarious (or group) bird and does not attempt to be. However, this isolation does not seem to bother the eagle. In fact, I think he rather enjoys it.

The other birds call to him but he pays them no attention. He cannot afford to be bothered with other birds that do not want to fly higher. It is not that he puts them down, but he is not content to fly from tree to tree or hop around on the ground in search of worms. For the eagle has experienced what other birds will never know —the power and swiftness of the jet airflows that he alone enjoys. His goal is to fly where the air is thin and the sun is bright.

While other birds sit and chatter among themselves, the eagle flies alone. He must, without exception, pursue what is instinctively in his heart. It is during this time that the eagle becomes a master of the wind, utilizing currents not available at lower altitudes.

Is this not a picture of the Eagle Christian, who will not submit himself to the nature of others who spend all of their time in activities of one sort or another and never learn the ways of the high winds of the Spirit? To really walk with God the Eagle Christian must pursue solitude, not as an escape, but rather to be alone with God and learn the ways of the Spirit of God. Leaving those things which lie behind the Eagle Christian presses on ever upward.

> "I do not consider brethren that I have captured and made it my own [yet] but one thing I do: forgetting what lies behind and straining forward to what lies ahead, I press on toward the goal to win the prize to which God in Christ Jesus is calling us **upward**." Philippians 3:13-14

The Eagle Christian is a heavenly creature who is called upward to meet and fellowship with his Creator. Yes it is a lonely life in the sense that others may not follow. It is lonely in the sense that he does not participate in many of the social functions, but it is not lonely in the sense that he has constant fellowship with life itself,

Photo: G. Wolf

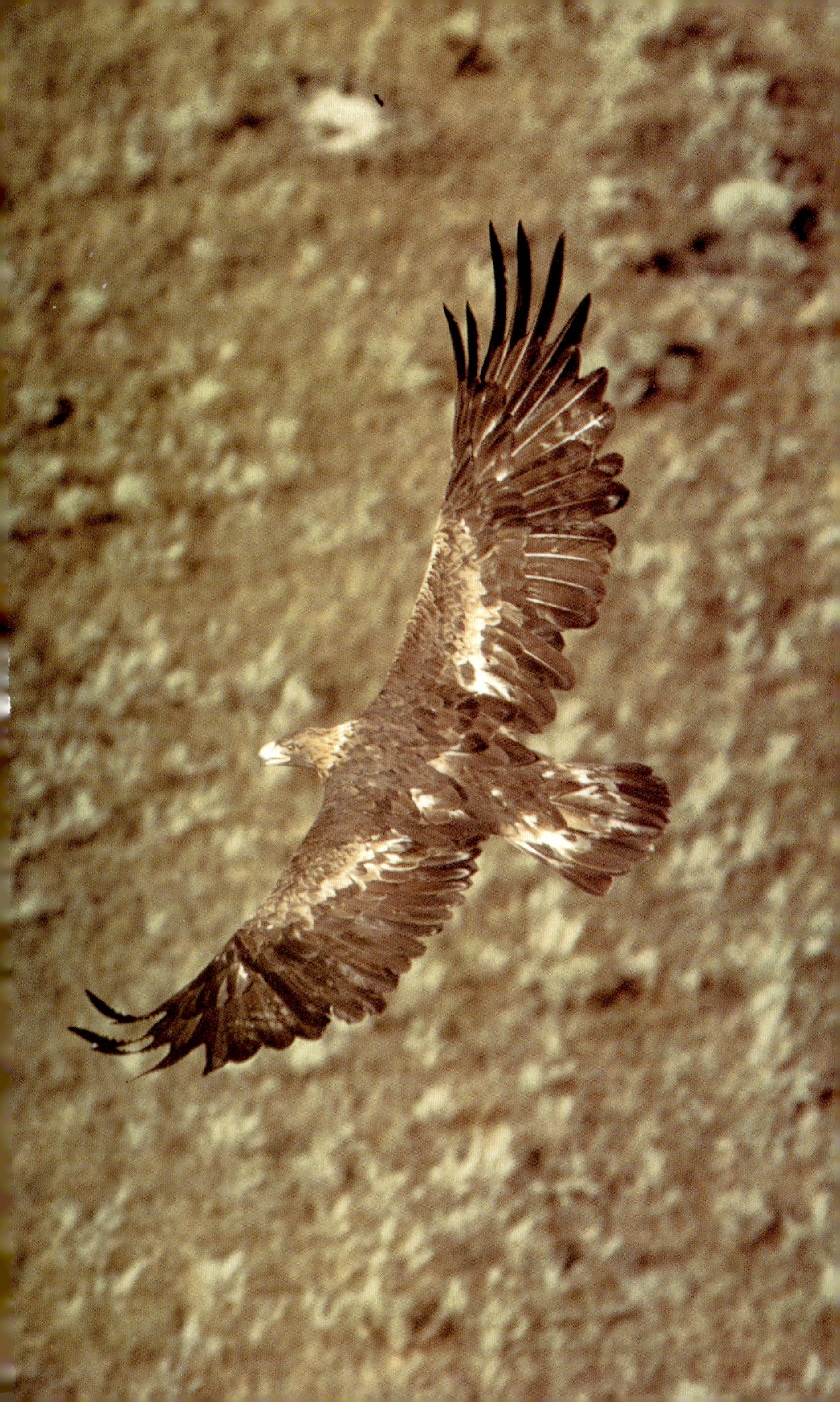

for Jesus is that life and only those who pursue the calling upward, separate from the world, will know intimacy with their Creator.

It is the eagle who stands before God's throne in the book of Revelation as though he were in flight, a representative of the nature of God and of those faithful servants who will pursue eaglehood.

> "And in front of the throne there is also what looks like a transparent glassy sea, as if of crystal. And around the throne, in the center at each side of the throne are four living creatures . . . **and the fourth living creature was like a flying eagle.**" Revelation 4:6-7

In my years of being a Christian I have known only a few men and women whom I could say had reached full maturity in the Spirit, and I have observed these people, I have noticed one common factor to which I can attribute their maturity and skillfullness. That common characteristic was their continual neglect of social (Christian and non-Christian) functions to be alone either in prayer, the study of the Word or in just plain worship of a God they are in love with.

This lonely creature (the eagle) may perhaps be an endangered species in the world today because they are so few. But I do not believe that there will ever be a day when there are not at least a few Eagle Christians who will soar in the presence of God and bask in the warmth of His glory.

> "Then I [looked and I] saw a **solitary** eagle flying in mid-heaven . . ." Revelation 8:13

The eagle perceives weather changes long before other animals due to his altitude and great eyesight. *Photo: U.S. Fish & Wildlife Service.*

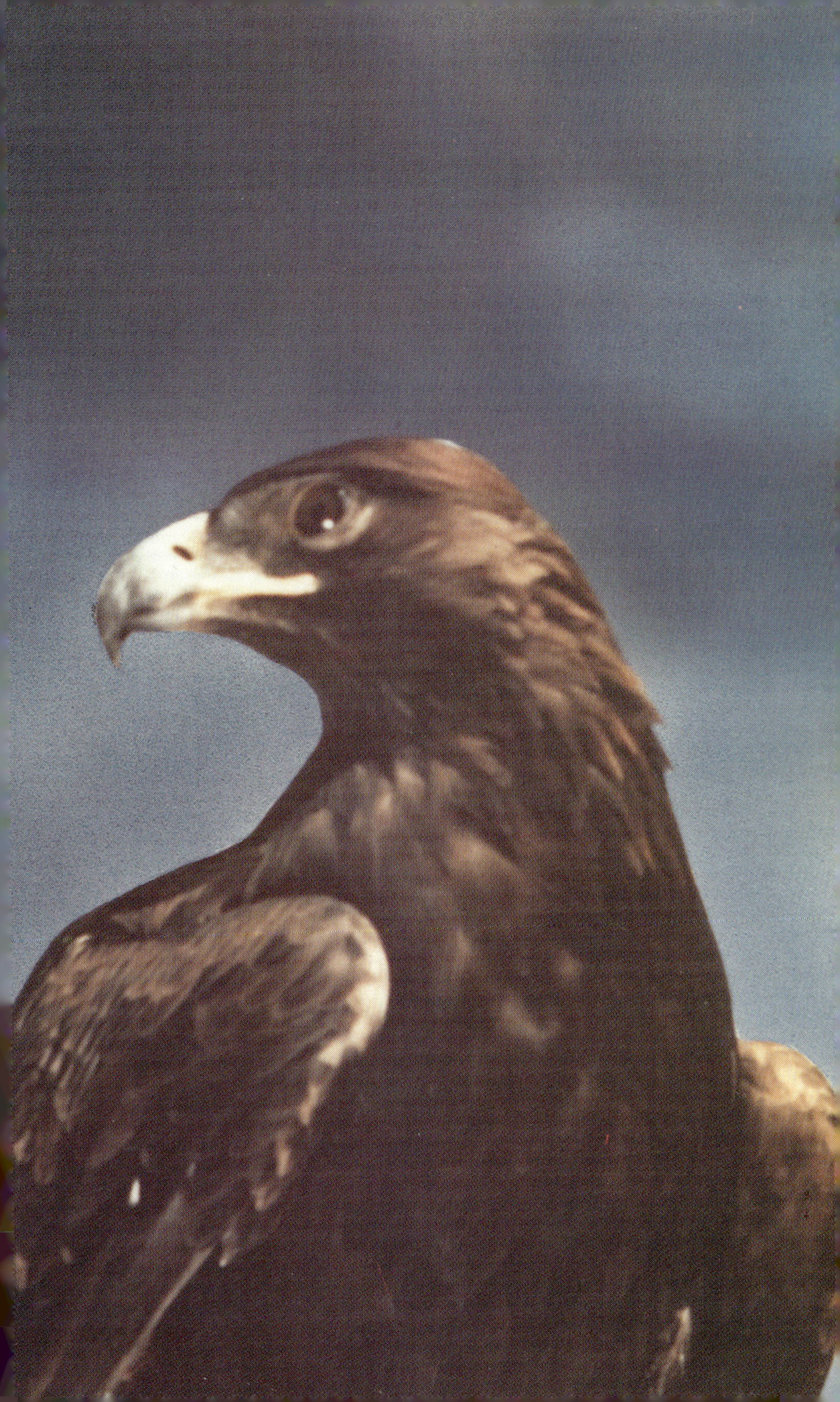

15
The Eagle in the Storm

Most animals by nature have the ability to sense the coming of a storm, some by smell and some by sight, and will instinctively search for shelter — rabbits to their burrows, bees to their hives and deer to their place of rest. However the eagle, because of his binocular vision, has the ability to see the storm approaching from a great distance. Yet he does not seek cover like the other wildlife. Instead, he sits on the side of his nest and awaits the storm. From his lofty perch he sees the other animals running for shelter, yet is himself unafraid of the storm although he has no power to stop the storm from approaching. Soon the high winds that accompany the storm begin to blow around the eagle, yet he is still unafraid. The clouds draw closer and closer and the eagle sits patiently until the first few drops of rain begin to fall round about him. The eagle launches flight from his lofty home and locks his wings in an ascending position. Using the strong winds that accompany the storm, he begins to spiral round and round, each time going higher and higher until at last he sees the sunlight beams around him and he looks down only to see the storm clouds pouring their rain on everyone but him.

If there are any young in the nest, mother eagle will remain behind, although she too has a desire to ascend above the clouds. Instead, she will open wide her wings (spanning from six to ten feet) and completely cover the brooding area. The young will peer out from under her wings only long enough to see their father disappear above the clouds.

The analogies here are so clear but I want to cover each one of them to be sure nothing is missed. First of all, let us take notice of the nature of "non-eagles." Let us suppose that the storm represents hardship, perhaps a battle for survival, or more generally, just a difficult time. It is the nature of "non-eagles" to run and hide yet the Eagle Christian experiences no fear whatsoever.

> Notice here how the mother opens her wings and offers warmth and shelter. You can also get a good idea of the size of the nest by the eight foot wingspan of the mother eagle.
> *Photo: G. Wolf*

Some "non-eagles" run to others for help, others simply run away. But the Eagle Christian knows long before the storm arrives that he is going up where the Son is always shining, above the dominion of the storm. The eagle, although fearless of the storm, does not have the ability to stop it, only to rise above it. There will be storms that confront the life of every Christian and non-Christian. There will be hard times and tribulation but God's intent is not to put fear in you or to chase you off or even to destroy you. God's intent is to allow you to do what no other species can do — conquer the storm by putting it (like the eagle does) under your feet.

The winds that accompany the storm are a special breed of their own. They are hard, fast and destructive, yet the master of the winds (the Eagle Christian) is not frightened but rather challenged by them. Each storm has its own separate wind currents, different from every other storm. And so does hardship that confronts the life of a Christian. This one factor alone has the ability to make a better "bird" out of you with each passing storm, until the storm is no longer a thing to be feared in you but rather a lesson to be learned, a foe to be conquered. Let the storms of life drive you to God.

And what of mother eagle who has sacrificially stayed behind to protect her young? What can be said of this? In my personal life I have seen God use others to cover me with their pinions (feathers) and shield me while the storms blew over. I have especially seen God cover me personally with His own pinions of protection. Like the mother eagle who takes the brunt of the storm upon herself, so Jesus took the impact of our sins upon Himself and shielded us from judgment which would surely have destroyed us.

At other times I have been used in the lives of young Christians to take the brunt of some storm. I could have flown away above the storm and let the younger ones fend for themselves, but God placed in the heart of an eagle the desire to protect the young — even sacrificially, and so He gave us the grace to endure what we must to become what He is changing us into.

"He will cover you with His pinions and under His wings shall you trust and find refuge . . ." Psalms 91:4

The majestic golden eagle in flight.
Photo: G. Wolf

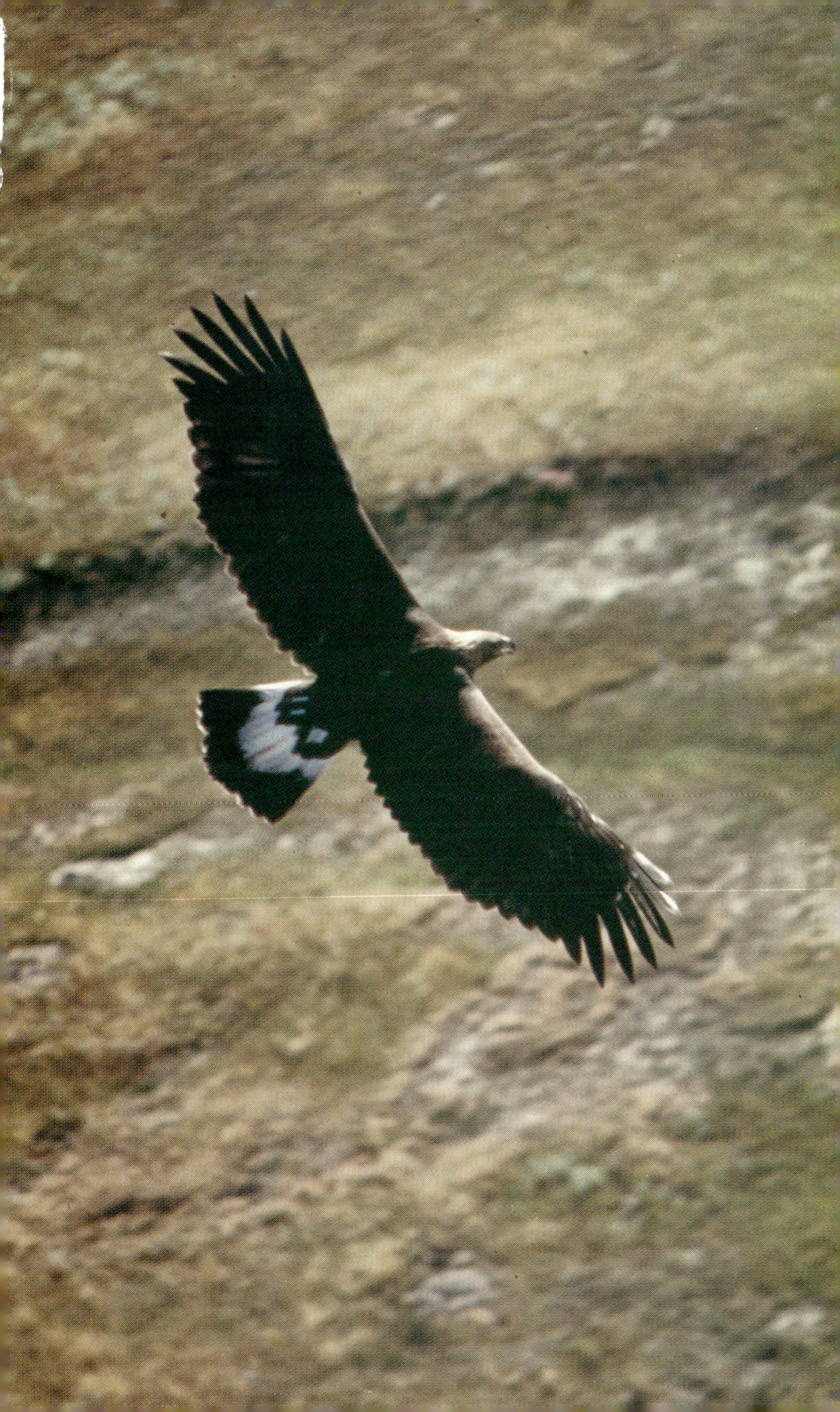

16
The Majestic Eagle

Undoubtedly the eagle is the King of Birds. His nature is truly a revelation of God, as the preceding chapters have plainly demonstrated. But there is one remaining characteristic of the eagle that points to God more than any other, and that is the majesty of the eagle in flight. Majesty is defined as the greatness and dignity of a sovereign and his grandeur. It is not a term that is used loosely with things of beauty, wealth or strength, but is reserved only for those who possess all these things and more.

The eagle, in flight, is all of these things. His mastery of the awesome force of the wind, his beauty in flight, his strength in battle, his compassion for the young and his all-encompassing eyesight are but a shadow of God.

The eagle, unlike other birds, does not wing flight by batting his wings for he knows that his ability to fly is not the result of his own strength but rather a gift of God. The eagle mounts the wind much the same way one mounts a horse and takes the reins in hand and controls his direction. Although he is subject to the wind, he also knows how to use the wind to reach some predetermined place. Years of flying have given to the eagle a knowledge that none other can have nor understand.

I was recently traveling to a speaking engagement with some brothers and sisters when someone pointed out the window and said, "Look, an eagle." With a real sense of anticipation we all glanced out the window. I took a look at the feathered bird and disappointedly advised them all that it was a hawk. In the aftermath of that disapointment, I sat wondering why the sighting of an eagle should cause such a stir. There is an innate desire in man to see majesty. Civilizations of all kinds have hailed the eagle and even sought to identify theselves with such a majestic creature as this.

The total isolation of the eagle, his setting himself apart from all others, as well as his freedom from natural forces such as gravity and his swiftness all say that the eagle is the most majestic of all creatures. And all of these things are possible to man.

As long as there has been sin, men have sought for freedom. As long as there has been a heaven, men have sought to fly. As long as there have been battles, men have sought to be fearless. As long as there have been obstacles of any kind, man has wanted to subdue them. This is majesty, the ability to reign and be lord of all. The psalmist wrote one of the most pictorial sketches of God ever written:

> "The Lord reigns; He is clothed with majesty; the Lord is robed, He has girded himself with strength and power; the world also is established, that it cannot be moved. Your throne is established from of old; You are from everlasting. The floods have lifted up, O Lord, the floods have lifted up their voice; the floods lift up the roaring of their waves. The Lord on high is mightier and more glorious than the noise of many waters, yes, than the mighty breakers and waves of the sea. Your testimonies are very sure; holiness is becoming to Your house, O Lord, for ever." Psalms 93:1-5

In Christ Jesus we have been called to be Eagles and to share in His majesty. Not to rob Him of glory but to reveal, as the eagles does, the glory of God to men. This is only possible to the Eagle Christian who has a master understanding of the winds of the Spirit of God.

> "The wind blows where it will; and though you hear its sound, yet you neither know where it comes from nor where it goes. So it is with everyone who is born of the Spirit." John 3:8

We need to learn the ways of the spirit of God in the same way the eagle learns the currents of the wind and reveals to man the majesty of an unseen force, the majesty of our Creator.

> "Oh Lord, our Lord, how excellent (majestic and glorious) is Your name in all the earth. You have set Your glory on [or above] the heavens." Psalms 8:1

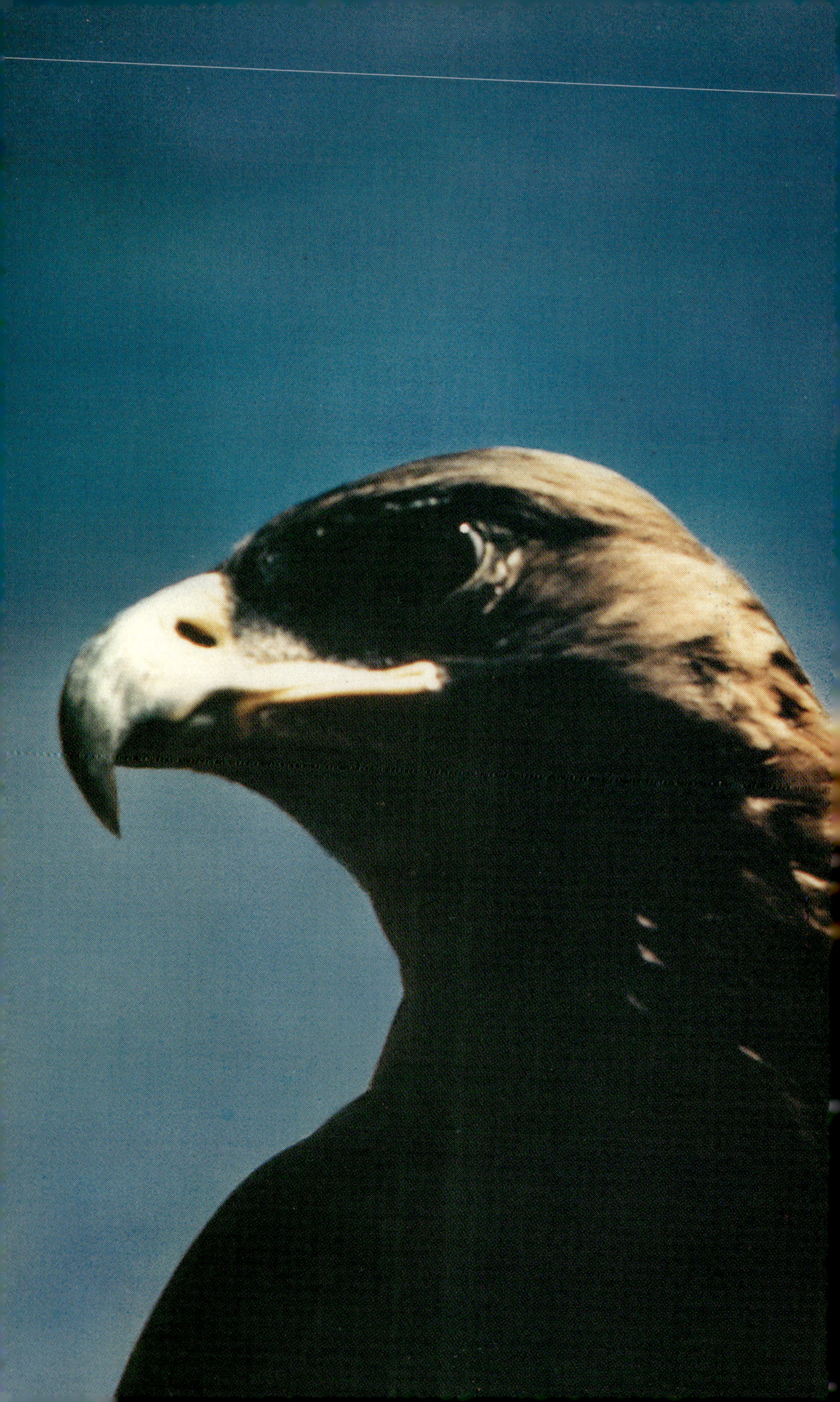

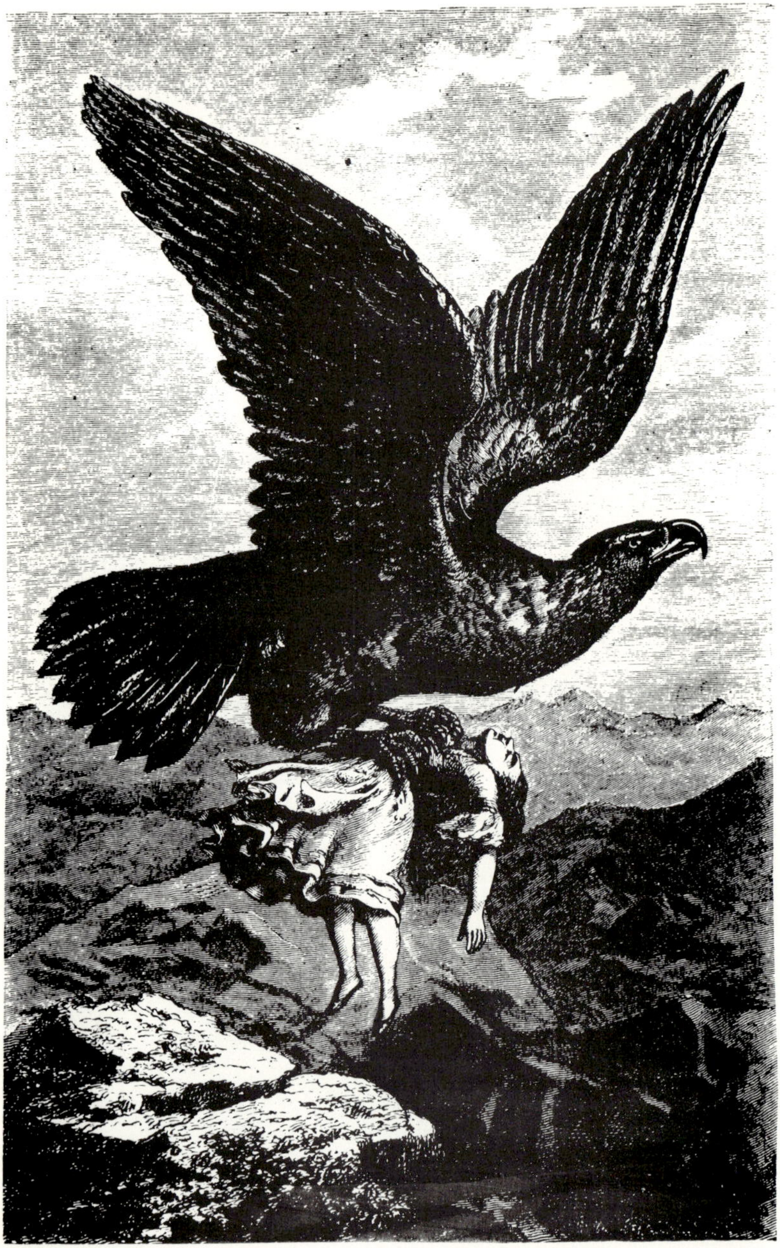

Encounter With An Eagle

The adjacent picture is a typical misconception of eagles. For centuries people believed that eagles would swoop down and snatch up young children and return to the nest and eat them. There is no evidence to support that story at all. The following story is the only known incident that would even suggest such an idea. In 1932 on a Sunday morning, June 5th, a young girl named Svanhild Hansen did have a very strange encounter with an eagle. While playing in her yard in Leka, Norway, Svanhild heard the sound of the eagle approaching. Before she could cry out for help the eagle clutched her dress and began carrying her off to his nest almost one thousand feet up above the valley floor.

Fortunately for Svanhild she weighed more than the eagle could carry, and the eagle dropped her on a mountain ledge some 800 feet up. The eagle was apparently trying to take her to his nest some 50 feet away.

Svanhild's parents had not seen the child being carried off but became suspicious as they saw the eagle continue to fly around the ledge where the child had been dropped. A search party and the girl's parents began a seven hour climb to the ledge where they believed the young girl to be. When they finally crested the ledge they found Svanhild asleep. With the exception of a few bruises and scratches, the child of four was alright. Svanhild kept her shredded dress which the eagle's talons had ruined and recently retold the story to a newspaper in Rorvik.

The stories that followed the publication of this strange encounter were so far out of proportion that people in many parts of the country became very aggressive toward birds of prey and began to deplete the eagle population. In the United States, especially in the western region, many sheep herders and hunters have killed vast numbers of eagles in the last few decades. Most of this has stopped now that eagles have been declared a protected species. Some states carry a $5,000.00 fine and one year imprisonment penalty.

The Years of the Eagle

Since the beginning of recorded history, the eagle has served as a symbol of power, freedom and immortality. The Egyptians used the eagle in their picture writing (hieroglyphics) and their priests made elaborate eagle masks for special religious ceremonies. Greek coins dating back to 413 B. C. were stamped with the images of eagles. Ancient astronomers, gazing at the stars, saw the outline of a soaring bird of prey and named the constellation "Aquila" (the Latin name for eagles). In Roman mythology, the symbol for Jupiter, king of the gods, was an eagle clutching thunderbolts in its talons.

Many Indian tribes of North America considered the eagle sacred. They used eagle feathers to decorate their ceremonial clothing and as rewards for acts of bravery performed in battle. Indians in the Northwest cared the figure of an eagle in their totem poles to represent a spiritual relationship between their families and this majestic predator.

On June 20, 1782, the Continental Congress adopted the bald eagle as the central figure of the Great Seal of the U.S.A. The District of Columbia and the states of New York, Pennsylvania, Mississippi, Missouri, Arkansas, Michigan, Iowa, Oregon, Utah, New Mexico and Wyoming also use the eagle in their official seal.

    —copy by J. Green
    taken from "The Years of the Eagle" Poster,
    National Wildlife Federation

ADDITIONAL INFORMATION

The average weight of a mature golden eagle is 31 pounds.

Eagles maintain their domain of about five to six square miles in sets of male and female.

The four stages of maturity are called: fledgling, post-fledgling, juvenile and breeding adult.

Eagles mate for life. A change of mate takes place only at the death of one or the other.

Eagles (except during child rearing) normally spend 4 to 6 hours per day in flight.

In a vertical dive an eagle can attain speeds in excess of one hundred to two hundred miles per hour.

Eagles continue to use the same nest year after year making some minor changes. Nest weight varies from one to two tons; nests are called eyres (or aeires).

Eagles norally feed on pests of human food supplies: hares, rodents and game birds.

Although they have the capability, they do not normally flap their wings.

Eagles do not migrate south unless food supplies are completely depleted.

Incubation of eggs averages 40 to 45 days.

The average nest of a golden eagle is built between six to ten thousand feet up, preferably in a cleft of rock.

The golden eagle ranks highest on the "evolutionary" tree. (The author does not agree with the evolutionary **theory**; however, it should be noted that science has rated the golden eagle at the top of the scale).

Eagles kill their prey with their talons (claws).

Eagle eyesight is eight times more powerful than man's, allowing them to see greater distances and colors. Their vision can be both monocular or binocular. This unique ability is due to two foreae or areas of high visual acuity.

The beak of an eagle is always hooked to aid in the tearing of flesh from prey which is held with the talons.

The eyesight and hearing of eagles are extremely acute; however, their sense of smell is not very good.

The male eagle is smaller than the female, giving her the ability to catch larger prey during the maturing of the young. This is also a benefit in her protection of them.

The male eagle is sometimes known as a tercel (eagles are also known as raptors).

Eagles do not prey on humans or animals much larger than small sheep. However, in extreme hunger they have been known to attack much larger animals.

The golden eagle (aquila chrysaetos) is of the family of Accipitridae. Found also under Falconidae.

The talons on a full-grown eagle are larger than the canine teeth of a lion.

The average wing span of a mature eagle is six to ten feet.

Greek coins dating back to 413 B.C. were stamped with images of eagles.

✓Preening is a one hour process performed every day by the eagles in which each feather is run through the mouth while breathing out to steam clean them. They also use an oil secreted in a separate gland to coat the feathers and make them moisture resistant. This is especially helpful when fish are a primary food source.

Hackels are long feathers on the neck and lower back which can be raised when the eagle is excited, much like the hair on a cat's back.

Scripture References

Proverbs 23:5

Isaiah 40:31

II Samuel 1:23

Jeremiah 4:13

Job 9:26

Job 39:27-29

Deuteronomy 32:9-12

Psalms 103:1-5

Ezekiel 1:10

Revelation 4:7

Revelation 8:13

Genesis 1:20-21

Exodus 19:4

Hebrews 3:1

Ephesians 2:6

Hebrews 4:12

Proverbs 4:20-22

Philippians 3:14

Psalms 91:1-10

Psalms 63:3

Proverbs 22:6

Proverbs 14:26

II Chronicles 16:9

Romans 8:37

Luke 10:19

II Corinthians 3:18

I Corinthians 2:14

Resources

The Life of Birds; Published by Alfred A. Knopf, Inc. New York, NY; Copyright 1962 W. B. Sanders Co.

Stefferud, Alfred
Birds in Our Lives; United States Government Printing Office, Washington D.C.; Copyright 1966

Durden, Kent
Flight to Freedom; Published by Simon & Schuster, New York, NY; Copyright 1974

Mannix, Dan
The Last Eagle; McGraw-Hill Book Company, New York, NY; Copyright 1965

The Interpreters Dictionary of the Bible; Abingdon, Nashville, TN; Copyright 1962

The New Encyclopedia Britannica; William Benton Publishers, Chicago, IL; Copyright 1984

Storer, Doug
Encyclopedia of Amazing but True Facts; Sterling Publishing Co. Inc., New York, NY; Copyright 1980

Welty, Joe Carl
The Life of Birds; Published by Alfred A. Knopf, Inc. New York, NY; Copyright 1962 W. B. Sanders Co.